ULRIKA

WISDOM BEYOND WHAT YOU KNOW

How to Shift from Being Driven by the Mind
to Living from the Heart and Intuition

ISBN Paperback – 979-8-9853416-1-4

Library of Congress Control Number – 2021924378

Printed in the United States of America.

Ulrika Sullivan
ulrika@ulrikasullivan.com

www.UlrikaSullivan.com

For my sister, Caroline.

Without knowing it, you nudged me in the right direction toward heart-centered living.

You were the first person who showed me a self-help book.
You were the first person who showed me the power of astrology.
You were the first person who showed me tarot cards.
You were the first person who listened when I had questions about it all.

I love you.

CONTENTS

INTRODUCTION

I n the midst of my professional corporate career, with a young family, I found myself very successful, highly valued, and overworked and unfulfilled.

I found myself standing in my messy kitchen late one cold winter evening, feeling totally stressed and drained because of the endless back-to-back meetings, juggling kids, activities, work travel commitments, the increasing home to-do list on millions of post-its, and ending the day in front of the computer to squeeze in some late night hours of work, but I carried on...

Fast forward to a few years later. It was a bright spring morning. I took a deep breath to inhale the fresh air. I was on my way to meet up with a good friend that I hadn't seen in a long time. As we sat down at the little cozy cafe and began to catch up, she stopped herself and looked at me mid-sentence. There was a slight pause as if she was searching for the right words. "There is something different about you, Ulrika. What is it? I can't put my finger on it."

I smiled and nodded slowly and looked back at her with a sense of inner recognition. I wasn't surprised that she had sensed something different about me, but I was happy she noticed. The last time we saw each other, I was late and rushed to see her; my thoughts were everywhere but the present. Now, as we sat here at a corner table, I felt calm and excited and I couldn't wait to tell her about it. And I can't wait to tell you...

This book will help you to make a conscious shift from being externally focused and driven by the mind to being internally focused, living from the heart and your intuition. It's an important, significant leap to make, a timely expansion of consciousness. This change will ultimately activate your ability to live a multidimensional life.

I intimately know the pressures of ambition in a mind-driven world that is pushing us to feel scattered and disconnected. I know exactly what it's like to ignore my own needs and just keep going *one more day*.

The difference I experience now is on the inside, not on the outside. It's not the joy of admiring a new perfect hair color or the sensation of putting on a perfectly fitted dress—things I used to associate with pleasurable emotions or outcomes. It's a new sense of ease, flow, self-empowerment, and inner calm that is unbreakable, no matter what.

There was a lot that happened for me along the way from being a stressed-out career mom to an intuitive spiritual life coach and energy healer.

Why Now?

For decades, our modern way of living has had a relentless focus on achievement based on seemingly tangible analytical and mind-driven measures, such as comparison, competition, and money.

It's an environment where some of us felt that we had to prove our worth to ourselves and others again and again. As a result of living a life driven by external success, we've been struggling to stay in inner balance and harmony.

We experience this nagging feeling of always being behind because the yearly goals changed (again!) and there is an unspoken expectation to "be flexible" and freely volunteer our time and energy, ignoring the potential consequences to our physical, emotional, and mental health, such as anxiety, depression, burnout, and adrenal fatigue to name a few.

This way of defining success can be seen as a culmination of a mind-driven world; a "go-go-go" lifestyle where multitasking, stress, and fully booked calendars are the norm.

With our minds in charge for so long, we have created a complicated tower of beliefs that are so far from what our hearts and souls are made of. As the Earth is evolving, and us with her, this tower of limiting beliefs created by the mind has got to transform.

In the past decades, we've put so much value in building physical evidence of success, but it has also resulted in the need to build barriers and walls within us to separate ourselves from each other; to show "who made it" and who did not. The walls some of us have built are made of destructive thoughts and behaviors that result in duality, a clear division of what is right and wrong; who's the winner and who's the loser; who has the power and who is powerless.

This vicious cycle was interrupted in early 2020 by the global COVID-19 pandemic. This event inadvertently caused many of us enter a period of deep soul searching to find stable ground.

A year later, the 2021 UN Happiness Report shared that trust was shown to be a key factor linking happiness to the effects of the ongoing pandemic.[1] The interesting thing about this study and its findings is that *trust* is a *belief*. It's heart energy. And trust can only be generated from within each of us individually. Trust is not something we can buy or compete to get.

It's an inner shift.

If you believe that now is the time to make a shift to step out of this exhausting duality, you're in the right place. The feeling coming from within of "There's gotta be MORE than this" is right on time.

We now have a great opportunity to open up and align with new ways of relating to both our life and what success is so that we can better stay in harmony and balance within ourselves, with others, and our environment. A supportive environment where no one's creativity and contributions are frowned upon or uncounted. A place where each individual is honored for their unique expression and talent. A space where we have nothing to fear, no anxiety-ridden mind battles to fight or soul power given away. An Earth of well-being and love. The opportunity we have now is to stop allowing our anxiety-filled stories that the ego mind has made up to influence us. We have the chance to reconnect with ourselves and with nature and to live in harmony with ourselves, others, and our environment.

We have the opportunity to stop sacrificing our body's health and the health of our relationships in order to uphold values that the past has ingrained in us about our success or our worth.

Moving forward, we're invited to critically analyze our inherited belief systems and how we use our minds.

Consequently, the definition of success is also destined to evolve. While collectively we still believe success comes from following a defined career path, we will eventually progress to a new definition — one that defines successful living as a life where one follows their unique soul path.

A shift is upon us. We're heading towards a new paradigm of multidimensional, heart-centered living. The time is now to let go of the long-held resistance and daily struggle that has held us back from

---

[1] John F. Helliwell et al., "World Happiness Report 2021," Last accessed Nov 2, 2021, https://worldhappiness.report/.

our true self-expression. The perception that our physical selves are the be all end all is coming to an end.

The hallmarks of heart-centered living include trusting our intuition, aligning with our true self, expressed through our life's work and life purpose, aligning with the energy flow of our natural environment, and listening to our body's wisdom.

When we align with our unique natural energy as individuals, we feel lighter. By learning how to notice synchronicities and receive intuitive guidance on a daily basis, we align with Universal guidance that is available to us, and we experience a clearer sense of the ever-present magic in every moment.

We are stepping into a time where we are invited to expand our awareness beyond the physical into trusting what we can't see, to eventually integrate a daily connection with the Universe to our human experience as our new normal. We're getting back in touch with our intuition and our body's wisdom and getting in touch with where our energy goes and how we use it.

The way energy is discussed in this book is from the perspective of how impactful it can be when we become aware of our own energy (and others' energy) and learn how to manage and direct our own energy on a day-to-day basis.

The benefits you will realize as we make this transformation are a greater sense of self-love, a feeling of self-empowerment, feeling wholeness when connected with your body and the Universe, living through your own wisdom, and experiencing effortless manifestation.

To break all of this down in a more concrete way, here are some potential practical scenarios you may experience as you are making a shift to heart-centered living:

* Spontaneous love for yourself and life as you wake up in the morning.
* Joyous exhilaration within as you share your truth with others.
* The full-body YES! when you just KNOW and go for it with no regret or doubt.
* The realization that a dysfunctional relationship taught you how to set boundaries and stand in your power.
* The inner knowing that success is coming with the patience to wait for it. Then, all of a sudden, it's HERE

The Framework

The book is divided into three parts.

In the first part, we'll examine some of the common mind-driven patterns we experience. The intention of this part of the book is to help you recognize how these patterns may impact your life today.

In the second part, we dive into heart-centered living and some of the fundamental aspects to consider. The intention with this part is to bring awareness to an expanded view of perception beyond the limiting patterns of the mind, as discussed in Part 1.

In the third part of the book, you will find seven shifts that outline the steps to making the transition from a mind-driven life to living from the heart and intuition. These shifts require *time* and *commitment* to fully realize but are essential to act upon continuously for expanded consciousness.

Following the stories and concepts presented in each chapter, a concluding exercise will help you to dive deeper, reflect on your own situation, and embed the principles outlined in the text.

How to Use This Book

I believe that we humans are wired to always grow and evolve through hard times. And I also believe in the good old saying: "Everything happens for a reason. Just believe." However, sometimes, we just need to make a major leap forward and catch up to the evolution that is going on. This book is such a catch-up moment.

I encourage you to read this book with curiosity and a "beginner's mind" as well as complete and implement the exercises in this book to get a deeper experience of the ideas and shifts that I'm suggesting.

I intend for this book to be part of a long-term experience, where the concepts in this book function as a catalyst and contribute to a life-long shift in perception and ultimately a brand-new lifestyle for you.

In addition to the investment of reading the book and using it as an interactive tool as you complete the exercises, I want this book to provide a simple gateway for learning. I also want you to take what you learn and act on it.

Ultimately, I want to help you make the shift from being driven by the endless stories of the mind to trusting your true self, your heart, and your intuition so you can turn here for direction and truth.

With this book, I'd like to inspire and encourage you to take responsibility for your own life balance and well-being and make the leap from being driven by the mind to living from the heart and intuition.

As you get familiar with, implement, and live these shifts, you may realize you're ready to commit to making a major leap forward. This major leap or "catch up" either comes voluntarily or it comes forced upon us out of the blue. In my case, it came out of the blue (as you'll learn about soon).

I hope that the stories from my own life have the inspirational power to launch you into your own transformation and shifts that are right for you. My stories may not look the same as your circumstances, but the energy shift is the same.

By contemplating and integrating the seven shifts described in this book, you have the potential to launch yourself into your next level of transformation. Only you know how a shift is going to express itself for you in the context of your life. However, these inner shifts are destined to happen as you evolve spiritually. There is a reason you're reading this right now.

Trust it.

My hope for you is that this book will inspire you to dive into your quest for a deeper understanding and experience of your current patterns in life that may hold you back from connecting with yourself through the dimensions of your true self, your energy, your body wisdom, your guides, and your inner voice as facilitated by your intuition for more ease and flow in your life so that you feel empowered to see your life in a new light.

Point of No Return

I felt my heart sinking in my chest as I sat on my simple but sturdy IKEA office chair. The silence was piercing. My body froze, my breath stopped, and my mind screamed. I couldn't utter a sound. I just sat there, staring at my screen with my earphones in.

I was paralyzed until someone on the other line said, "Are you still there?"

I managed to stutter, "I'm here. Can you tell me again what just happened?"

At that moment, rage set in. I could feel my body temperature rise dramatically, and my insides were shivering. Thankfully, I could almost hold back my tears, but it was obvious I was in shock. It was so hard to even say anything without losing it.

Instead of succumbing to my anger, I went on the polite defense. "Was there no way you could have given me a head's up about this? How come these changes to the group are completely news to me? I am COMPLETELY surprised, I must say, and I didn't expect this AT ALL." I caught my courage in the moment to say, "I am very disappointed in how this was handled."

The human resource person was speaking. I didn't hear it. She was likely repeating what she already had said before.

My boss said, "OK, that's all we had to say," and they both hung up. The teleconference was open with me on the line. I felt a complete silence both on the line and within me. I thought to myself, *What the F$%^ just happened?*

I was shaking as I put the phone down, with the line still open. I was staring at my screen with the upcoming year's objectives and goals document wide open since they were due to my boss tomorrow. There was a heaviness present that made me unable to move. I just sat there.

But inside me, there was chaos. It was like the Universe was screaming at me, "You're blind to what needs to change in your life, so we're going to carry you out, NOW."

After a few minutes, I reluctantly picked up the phone to call a friend and colleague. Without hesitation, I dove into what I wanted to say, "Do you know what just happened? I got released from my job! Can you believe it?!"

The deep rage I felt on the call with my boss and the human resources woman was still very real. I just had to get it all out, say things just the way I wanted to say them, and so I did, while half crying.

After twenty minutes or so of dissecting, word for word, exactly what had been said during the short call, my very patient and compassionate colleague said, "You'll be fine, Ulrika. Just find another job."

WHAT??

"NO, it's NOT just finding another job," I said. *As if it's something just to be picked up like that!* "You don't understand. I am not here anymore. I am lost. I am shrunk to a single breadcrumb. I'm not here. I just lost...ME!!"

I'd never felt like this in my life, ever.

Yes, I had been through bad breakups and heartbreaks over relationships multiple times in the past, but not like this.

I felt like my identity was gone.

In one phone call.

Later that day, another friend was trying to comfort me. I've always trusted her opinion, so I told her the entire story. I felt I had to go into every single detail about how this all played out and how surprised and devastated I was that something like this could happen to me.

Patiently, she reflected on the whole ordeal, and she said something that jolted me awake, "Listen, Ulrika, the truth is that you wouldn't have moved from there anyway. You weren't happy," she said.

I knew she was right. It made me feel somewhat better.

Maybe I needed a change. Maybe.

In the weeks that followed at work, I felt like I was floating free like a balloon in the sky with no direction. Like an undefined entity not belonging anywhere.

I dialed in to the last meeting with my team on a Friday morning. For everyone else, it was just another meeting, but I had been dreading it. It felt like I wanted to hang on to the last straw of familiarity.

I remained quiet for most of the meeting, which was unusual for me. On the surface, I felt empty and still shocked at what had happened a few weeks prior. There was seemingly no change for anyone else on the call.

As I completed my last meeting with my employer, I felt a sinking feeling in my stomach. Everything got quiet in my office, and I thought,

The Universe has made it 100 percent clear to me that I have attached my entire identity to my career! Immediately after this realization, another thought came into my consciousness: *So WHO AM I now without my job? I have NO idea!*

I had been completely caught off guard. However, deep down in my subconscious, I wasn't surprised by the past week's turn of events. It was clear that it was time to make a complete inner shift, from a life driven by the mind, multitasking, distracted, and disconnected—a life on autopilot—to a life led by the heart, connected, inspired, and fulfilling—a life guided by my inner voice. I couldn't ignore my inner nudges anymore.

My conscious ego had shown up surprised. *How could this all be happening?* Honestly, I realized my ego mind was late to the party, with no option to keep going within the comfort zone.

I thought to myself, *This time, I wasn't supposed to "miss" the message from the Universe, was I?* Many times before, I had probably just ignored the Universe's invitation to ask myself, "What's going on?" and listen for the answer. Now it was time for me to stop, listen, acknowledge my soul's call for change, and start asking myself the hard questions and truly listen to the answers.

So here I was, sitting at my desk, thrown out into complete uncertainty with a sinking feeling in my stomach completely paralyzing me.

There was something about this whole situation that hit me right in my core. I'd always wanted to be in control and be right. In my younger years, I was told repeatedly, "Why do you always need have to have all the answers, Ulrika?"

Uncertainty to me was like not having fuel in the car. Without some sort of certainty, I was not going anywhere. I was staying where I was, even if it wasn't good for me.

This time it was different. The Universe had stepped in to answer the call for change.

A few days later, I was sitting at the kitchen table after dinner, having turned the situation inside and out with my husband at length. As I stood up and walked toward the sink to put my empty teacup down, I said to my husband, "What if this negative situation is turning out to be something positive after all?"

"Yes, you never know," he replied. "It may be the best thing that ever happened to you."

As reluctant as I was to admit it, I knew he might be right.

Do I want to stay stuck going back in my old ways and continue on autopilot, or should I act and go in a completely new and uncertain direction?

Clearly, the Universe had answered my soul's call by literally pushing me (with force!) out of my job so that I finally opened my eyes. But I was still hesitant because it wasn't obvious (to my ego) that leaving a successful career behind me would be the best move. Ugh!

This flip-flopping mind game exhausted me. But the more I spent time thinking about what had happened with my job, the more it became clear that when the Universe is involved in revealing our next step on our journey, it's a plea to PLEASE answer the call!

So what did I do? I got honest with myself and started to ask myself more questions than I had never asked myself before.

Who am I now?

What do I want?

What do I not want?

What can I do?

What can't I do?

It was harder than I thought. I didn't have an answer to any of the questions I asked myself. I only knew the answers I comfortably had before, but those didn't help.

But I very soon realized that it felt good to ask myself those questions. It felt like going on an adventure. An adventure to discover myself and who I was without the identity that my job and long career had provided.

This self-directed adventure felt like a completely new discovery. I had no idea where it would take me, but deep down there was a spark of excitement. It felt like untapped ground on the inside of me. But the next moment, I would be feeling this endless pull into the void again, like I had lost my stability and identity.

Months later, I walked into the newly opened yoga studio in town. My yoga teacher suggested to me, "Have you thought of joining the yoga teacher training? We're starting in October. I think you'd be a great fit for the program."

"I hadn't thought of being a yoga teacher, so I don't know...." I said to her as we were chatting after class. The idea of deepening my practice enticed me, but becoming a yoga teacher? *No way. I can't do that!* I thought on the way home.

My still very logic-driven and conditioned mind kept telling me that anything new and therefore uncomfortable was not worth pursuing.

Nevertheless, I did sign up for the yoga teacher training. And somewhere inside me, I felt drawn to it as my subconscious knew that this would be one of the first synchronicities happening in answering the call.

I had practiced yoga in the past but had taken a few years' pause, as the kids were young and needed a lot of attention. I noticed that coming back to yoga was different this time. Now I opened up to the spiritual experience of the yoga practice instead of just viewing yoga as a form of physical exercise.

As I walked into the studio on a Friday morning, starting the yoga teacher training taking place over the next eight months, I didn't know anyone except the yoga teacher herself. And after a long but utterly wonderful weekend of yoga, I told one of my classmates, "It's like coming home!" I noticed that it felt so right to be there.

Connecting deeper spiritually with myself left me with a feeling of divine timing taking place. I felt free when connecting my inner spirit and my body during those weekends we were at the studio. Three days in a row, immersed in yoga philosophy, anatomy, and sequencing. Exhilarating! And exhausting!

I had never felt exhausted and exhilarated at the same time. Always just exhausted.

Through the energy of being with like-minded people, we get validated within ourselves. I noticed that I loved the energy in class, and I noticed how I felt so free and present. The inner experience during the yoga teacher training became a way for me to reclaim a part of me that I had lost. After being on autopilot for many years, I experienced my whole self for the first time in a long time!

Along with the yoga teacher training, we had to start teaching yoga (of course), and I found myself reconsidering. A growing part of me saw myself as a yoga teacher, despite all the self-doubt that I was still carrying within me. However, I struggled with my thoughts. *Can I really DO this?*

What I noticed was that everyone else had the same struggle of self-doubt and insecurity. *But maybe I can do this after all?! Yes! I CAN! I AM doing it!* I told myself and graduated the following month, proudly holding my diploma.

The yoga teacher training was the start of my journey to self-awareness and realizing how incredibly integral the body-mind-spirit connection truly is to hear our soul's truth and guidance

One evening, a year later, when I was in a Facebook group scrolling around, I came across a conversation about coaching.

My eyes stopped at a question someone had asked about coaching certifications and how to become a life coach. Something within me said, *Ha! Interesting!* I read some more responses further down in the post. One person had posted a link to a reputable international life coach school, and I clicked the link.

I browsed the website, and I immediately felt an inner pull and energy rising within me. Without much thought, I signed up to be contacted.

Signing up right away was out of character for me, but my inner voice was so loud about this that I knew it was something I had to look into further.

Even before I got on the phone with the coaching company, I felt that feeling again of "I have to do this." Hence, it wasn't surprising that I came up with the investment and signed up to become a certified professional life coach.

The coaching training was everything I had hoped for and more, and I began to think that it was something that I could do as a profession.

In the back of my head, I was toying with the idea of having my own business. However, very present in my reality was the fact that I "should have" a very high-paying job and stable income, vacation days, and everything that comes with employment. *Is it even realistic to think that I could do coaching for a living?* I wondered.

The further I got in the training, the more I started to listen to my inner voice *Hmmm, this is what I need to do next...!!* This feeling became strong and felt like a reality. I started to believe in it more and more.

One day, during my life coach training, we did a very powerful exercise where we were asked to identify a common sentence that our ego-mind voice kept telling us.

The sentence from my ego-mind voice was: "I'm too shy to have a successful business." Then, we were asked to let go of the ego mind's voice and instead invite a different energy, through our heart, and a message directly sourced from our true self.

Immediately, the feeling of contentment came over me as I spoke the words that I heard within me: "I am an abundant, gifted, spiritual teacher, coach, and guide."

I could feel the power of those words from my heart space, and my body relaxed. I believed the words instantly because they were *me*.

From there on, I was guided by an inner feeling of "point of no return," a deep connection to my inner voice, my heart's desire, and body consciousness that I had never experienced before. There was no going back.

This was the pivot I had subconsciously waited for that would provide me with an opportunity to fully step into self-empowerment and communion with the Universe for inner and outer transformation.

There has never been a question since.

That feeling of autopilot was forever gone, as I can go to my heart for confirmation instead of trying to figure it out with my ego mind's logic.

What I decide to spend my energy on now is my life's work, and I am the engine pulling the train.

I'm sovereign and self-empowered.

I didn't know then how right I was. But I did listen to my inner voice to pursue coaching as a profession.

Leaving a very long career in the corporate world to become an entrepreneur felt like starting as green as a sprout in the spring. It was indeed a leap of a magnitude that I'd never thought I'd be making.

But the funny thing is I never hesitated once. I knew this was what I was meant to do.

I call it my "point of no return" feeling.

It was a feeling I had never felt before. It's a full-body feeling. It comes straight from the heart, and the body is entirely on board, no matter what the mind says.

There is no way to doubt that feeling. It just is. It's a body response.

It's the real deal because I didn't have to ask anybody else what the answer was. I just knew. No conditions.

It just HAD to happen.

So I started my business as an intuitive spiritual life coach.

A bright morning, months later, I began my day by reflecting upon how I had changed since that "point of no return" feeling and when it became clear to me that I was heading in a completely new direction that had to do with coaching.

I asked myself, *What is the difference now?* The thought that came to me was, *I feel passion for my life again, and I can feel myself smile with my entire being.*

My thoughts continued, and I wrote in my journal. "The passion I know now and that is present in my experience of life today is not dependent on anyone else or what I do. What I feel in my life today is universal energy flowing through me instead of struggling and trying to work against it."

I realized that the morning routine I developed had helped me discover a new level of self-love. It had taken me months of regular practice in conversation with my inner voice, turning my energy to my inner world every morning.

I looked up to the ceiling and felt into the experience of the past months as if I was trying to put a word to the experience. What came to me at that moment was the insight that when I tap into and feed the energy of self-love, a change comes to my inner conversation as well.

I continued writing in my journal, "It's evident that when my inner conversation changes to a more supportive voice, I feel that passion and inner life force bubbling up. I am no longer chasing passion as a moving target, something I have to accomplish. Instead, the inner passion of self-love is right here within me, and it's not going anywhere."

As I wrapped up my morning meditation and prepared for half an hour of yoga, I felt grateful knowing that once I allowed myself to step out of my mind and stop struggling, the Universe was there to embrace me unconditionally through self-love and the passion I felt for my life.

The best news was that this newfound passion was not connected to what I produced or accomplished on a day-to-day basis. It was much bigger than that.

I was on a mission!

A few years later, I am now deep into my new path as a spiritual teacher and coach, making a complete shift from those stressful years (and mornings) to a life in tune with my inner voice.

Most mornings, I walk back into my bedroom, closing the door behind me. I gently close my eyes, and I exhale.

Aaahhhhhhh!

It's a deep exhale of freedom. It feels like all my life's burdens just suddenly fall off my shoulders every time I sit down on my yoga mat. It feels like I've stepped into a space of possibilities and calm energy just by closing the door, knowing I won't be disturbed for an hour. It's my precious morning time that I treasure more than anything else these days.

As I make myself the first cup of coffee of the day from the little coffeemaker I have in my bedroom, I feel like I'm stepping into a magical space of rejuvenation and cleansing.

I reach for an essential oil from the little wooden stand next to the coffee maker. I choose uplifting citrus and put a couple of drops in my diffuser. As I push the button on the diffuser, a soft purple light comes on, and the vapor starts to emerge. It smells heavenly from the notes of orange and some peppermint that I put in as well. The perfect combo to wake up to. I tip the bottle one more time as I put a drop on my wrists, rub both together, and inhale the fresh, uplifting aroma.

Then I light a candle, jump into my bed, and put a pillow behind my back against the headboard. Today I put my legs in an easy pose. Naturally, another deep breath is coming to me. Aaah…!

I feel the stillness in the room. I look out the window and see the early morning rays of sunlight come through.

This time of day is when I connect with myself and go deep. In this space of possibility, I can be in communion with my true self, my energy, and the Universe all at the same time.

In this space, no thought or action is predetermined or planned. There is no to-do list or next thing I have to do. Instead, it's a space of creativity, being here now, and a lightness of energy.

I pick up my phone. I find my list of favorite meditations and visualizations. I ask the Universe to show me a meditation that would serve me and the Earth best today. My thumb lands on a guided meditation, and I press play.

Surrounded by a soothing voice and the inner energy of unlimited creativity, I tap into my unbounded soul in communion with the Universe, observing where it takes me.

I invite images of travel between the cosmic and the earthly. The meditation is helping me tune in to the depths of my true self and tune out from the day-to-day and the physical reality of being in a room with four walls.

At the end of the meditation, I reach for my journal and pen. I ask a question to my spirit guides, and I immediately start to write whatever comes to me. I continue to let myself become one with the space between the spoken word and imagery.

My inner voice is speaking to me now, and I feel the message coming through the second I ask the question. It's a millisecond response when an inner knowing is coming through, sometimes as an image and sometimes words.

I write it down as soon as I get the message. This is because I want to document it, know it for later, but also so that my eyes can read it to process the message even further.

My inner voice is free flowing. I don't know what's coming through next. I wait. I sit in the space of possibility, waiting, and another message comes through with an instant image and words that I write down as if my hand is my thought.

Then I wait again. My eyes are closed, and I'm listening.

My inner knowing knows if there's more or if it's the end of this message stream.

"What else?" I ask.

Another message comes up, something completely different this time. Another message stream has emerged.

Different imagery and inner words are coming through. My mind is on pause, and instead, my body's wisdom has taken over the interpretation. Advice on the matter is coming through. The message is, "You are on the right path. Keep going."

My inner voice is always kind, loving, encouraging, and direct in its language. There is a sense of truth and matter of fact-ness, but what's coming through is always supportive and loving.

The messages are full of symbols, and there is great potential for interpretation based on the imagery that emerges within. The words that come through via my inner voice are clear, and they easily flow down on the page through my pen. I draw a big heart, thanking my inner voice for the messages. A warm feeling of gratitude emerges within me as I draw the heart, and I feel myself coming back into my reality.

As I sit on my bed, I think that this opportunity—to be with my true self, inner voice, and spirit guides (and other energetic beings)—that I'm giving myself daily is a way to learn how to relate to the unseen world. It's a way of giving and receiving that we all can be part of in addition to our day-to-day world of Earth and matter.

Another morning of feeling rejuvenated and lighter in my body, mind, and soul. I am ready for a new day.

This serene start of a morning would have never happened in the past, but now it is a natural part of how I approach each day.

Fortunately, the experience of living a stressful, multitasking life on autopilot was not the end of the story for me. I had ignored the patterns of exhaustion and disconnected from my body's wisdom, completely ignoring my need for balance and harmony. None of which I had conscious knowledge of that day as I was sitting on my office chair as I picked up the phone to answer that surprise call. A call that, in hindsight, came to me as a symbol of inevitable change that catapulted me from what I knew best and threw me out into the dreaded unknown.

I was given an opportunity to heal patterns that were not serving me and expand into a greater understanding of myself and higher consciousness.

I learned to trust my inner voice, body wisdom, and heart energy, deciding to put the multitasking and exhausted ego mind in the back seat, and ultimately found self-love through sticking to my daily spiritual practice. Through yoga, coaching, energy healing, daily meditation, and journaling, I got to know myself all over again and connect with the parts of me that I had disconnected from.

I learned what my natural talents and gifts truly were as an intuitive spiritual guide, coach, and healer. I'm getting to know what matters to me now: life balance, self-love, and service to others. By deepening the expression of who I truly am, I can decide what my values and boundaries are moving forward.

I went from being entirely driven by the mind, a product of the distracted ego, where my self-worth was influenced by a harsh inner critic, to being led by my ever-present, loving inner voice of guidance. Instead of being driven by what I can tangibly accomplish, what others think of me, or what others say is the right way to succeed, my inner voice of guidance provides a steady flow of gentle nudges, inner calm, and self-love—all of it within an unbreakable invisible shield of protection around me.

Today I know there is more to our existence than what we can see and measure. Now, living a life led by the heart, I no longer have to prove anything. A weight within my heart has lifted. I feel energized! No more exhaustion. There is nothing more I have to do or figure out. Today I know that I'm here to create effortlessly.

You, too, have an opportunity to connect with your inner knowing for more ease and flow in your life. It may not come as an unexpected phone call as in my case, but you'll know when that undeniable "point of no return" feeling is felt deep within your body. Then it's your turn to choose to listen to your inner voice of guidance.

PART 1
Mind-Driven Living:
The Re-Run Patterns

"The great dilemma with transforming consciousness is trying to reason with the mind that though it may be interesting, it should not be in charge of guiding the life. This is an enormous challenge."

— Ra Uru Hu

Our minds prefer to repeat past learning because the past is what the mind knows and draws its logic from. We were all given values in childhood and were shown how life was supposed to be lived and how success was to be defined. The mind keeps repeating these norms we adopted over and over again. Some of these patterns, which we may not even be personally aware of (yet!), contribute to us feeling stuck, stagnant, and unfulfilled. When our life patterns are working against our own soul's natural energy, we may feel frustrated or even trapped.

In the following chapters, you'll get an opportunity to recognize some of the patterns that are commonly repeated by someone who's living driven by the mind.

1. Working Hard for Success

We have a basic need to feel safe and in control of our lives. In our modern world, one way to create security is by working long, hard hours. Striving for success is a way to feel like we're in control. In Chapter 1, you will reflect upon the pattern of working hard as it relates to basic needs and the definition of success. You'll increase your awareness of how these patterns are playing out in your life and the perception of how well your own basic needs are met.

2. Pushing Yourself and Ignoring Your Needs

In the past, many of our ancestors had to go beyond their personal limits to survive. This survival pattern has subconsciously continued in modern living but may involve more complex situations than basic survival. In Chapter 2, you'll reflect upon the pattern of pushing yourself and ignoring your needs to increase your awareness for self-care and life balance.

3. Worrying About What Others Will Think

The common pattern of self-judgment, comparison, and worrying about what others will think is holding us back from our true potential. In Chapter 3, you'll reflect upon the pattern of worrying about external matters and increase your awareness of how it may impact your satisfaction with yourself and your life.

WISDOM BEYOND WHAT YOU KNOW

4. People Pleasing

People pleasing keeps our mind externally focused. In Chapter 4, you'll reflect upon the pattern of people pleasing and increase your awareness of how it may impact your perception of self-worth and your self-confidence.

5. Driven by the Ego

We all have an ego. One of the things that the mind is occupied with is the ego's constant stories. In Chapter 5, you'll reflect upon the pattern of being driven by the ego to increase your awareness of the ego's inner dialogue.

1

Working Hard for Success

"You get what you focus on."
— David Justus

It was a windy Tuesday morning in August. My mom held my hand as we walked towards the back door of the local bank where she worked. She brought me with her that day because my grandmother wasn't available to watch me as she normally did. My mom, an outgoing, headstrong, natural leader who had quickly advanced in the ranks at the bank, determinedly turned the key to the door, and we stepped into the dark hallway.

As we entered the building, its familiar back office made me feel happy and filled me with anticipation. I loved being at the bank with her.

The bank was about to open. Everyone at the bank was dressed up; the men were wearing suits, and the women were wearing nice dresses or skirts. I loved the idea that you looked more important if you dressed up. My mom also dressed up very nicely all the time. I wanted to work at the bank when I grew up.

We passed the bank's public area, where customers could stand or sit as they waited for their turn to go into my mom's office. "You can come to sit with me out in the public area today. I'm seeing a customer in a few minutes," she said. All of a sudden, six-year-old me felt so grown up and important. I was sitting next to her while she was seeing the first customer!

After a while, she turned to me and said, "Ulrika, can you walk this important paper over to Elizabeth? Make sure you get her signature."

"Of course, Mom," I said and smiled proudly. With my head held high and quick steps, I delivered the important paper to one of her colleagues across the public area.

Upon my return, as always, my mom praised me. "You are such a good girl!" I felt happy inside being so important in her life. I wanted to be like my mom. Her values around work seemed important. Visiting with her at work at an early age, I subconsciously absorbed her desire to work hard. Her ability to tolerate stress had already made a big impression on me.

A Role Model

I grew up in Småland, a rural area of southern Sweden, which is historically an area with the most frugal, stubborn, entrepreneurial, and resilient people. People here are known to work hard, and doing a "good job" at any cost was deeply ingrained in everyone, including me.

I often felt like I was in the shadow of my successful, outspoken, and opinionated mom. She was of the opinion that she knew what was best for me (and she probably did at the time), from my clothing choices to my hairstyle.

Honestly, I really didn't have to make one single choice for myself if I didn't want to. I just had to turn to Mom, and she had an answer for me without blinking.

However, with answers readily provided by her through the years, there was a growing lack of inner understanding of what I preferred, or what my own opinion was to form my own self-expression. This void within made me insecure about what I valued and it didn't support me to take a stand and set boundaries around what I liked and didn't like.

I just went with what others liked. As a teenager, my mind thought it was great just to follow and not have to have an opinion.

But my heart suffered…

With this pattern of being a follower, it was easy for me to take on new roles and interests in life. I was always seen as someone willing to learn and was on top of things and I was labeled ambitious in school. I was always available to take on another task if someone asked me.

I had carried forward my role of the "good girl working hard" from childhood, trying to get the praise to know I was good enough. Taking on this persona was the ultimate stage to be seen and validated.

This was also the start of a lifelong life pattern of associating my self-worth with success at work. As I began my professional career and started a family, this pattern of working hard and doing a good job continued, as it was expected by myself and seemingly everyone around me. I had to uphold my perceived self-worth. But it came at a high price.

My own life balance and well-being.

Success Redefined

In the past decades, society has valued hard work and overtime as something to be praised and rewarded. The term workaholism was coined in 1971 and is defined as "being overly concerned about work, to be driven by strong and uncontrollable work motivation, and to spend so much energy and effort into work that it impairs private relationships, spare-time activities, and/or health."[2]

In addition, for women who wanted to have a professional career alongside a family, the on-the-job and domestic work hours in total added up beyond the recommended eight-hour workday, which adds to the sensation of stress in life.[3]

The term work-life balance has been recognized since the 1970s and 80s, but in the early 2000s, the culture of working long, hard hours and tolerating stress became even more commonplace and soon became the best sought after trait you could have as an employee as described in a job description.

In addition, technology has made it possible for workers to be available twenty-four hours a day has continued to be another way that drives us to use our logic and analytical abilities of the mind to react to the instant information flow that is presented to us.

Leadership author Dr. Stewart Friedman, a professor at the University of Pennsylvania's Wharton School of Business, found in his studies related to leaders, leadership, and the definition of success that if someone puts

---

[2] Megan Hull, "Work Addiction Statistics," The Recovery Village, Last accessed Nov 2, 2021, https://www.therecoveryvillage.com/process-addiction/work-addiction/work-addiction-statistics/.

[3] Ceri Parker, "It's Official: Women Work Nearly an Hour Longer than Men Every Day," World Economic Forum, Last accessed Nov 2, 2021, https://www.weforum.org/agenda/2017/06/its-official-women-work-nearly-an-hour-longer-than-men-every-day/.

their self-worth in status, paycheck, and prestige, it can result in a less than fulfilling life, with a sense of lack of balance in relationships and emotional, physical, and spiritual aspects of life as a result.[4]

But, in the last decade, there have been glimmers of hope. For example, Generation Z has shown us that they are not willing to negotiate away a desired lifestyle and balance in life for a job that requires work hours beyond what they're willing to put in.[5] In addition, the "Success Project Survey" survey conducted by Streyer University in 2014 indicated that a whopping 90% believe that success is more about happiness than power, possessions, or prestige.[6]

Some early trends also indicate that some of us who are currently employed may consider a transition to entrepreneurship or self-employment due to factors such as the ownership of one's time and the perception of freedom and flexibility. In a survey by Dartmouth College cited by 20somethingfinance.com in 2021 indicates a 10:1 ratio of Americans that want to be self-employed versus those that actually are.[7]

The pattern of working hard for success is very relevant because it has to do with our basic needs. And that makes the pattern quite hard to redefine in our minds unless we can see the alternatives clearly.

Many people feel stuck in their jobs, or devastation following the loss of a job, and have a hard time finding alternatives if they have a belief that working hard equals success.

But as we start to redefine and widen the perspective of what success is, we have the opportunity to break free from past expectations of conformity and individual accumulation to create a definition of success that is rooted in harmony and balance, not only for ourselves but also for our community and environment.

---

[4] Stewart D. Friedman, *Total Leadership: Be a Better Leader, Have a Richer Life* (Boston: Harvard Business Review Press), 2008.

[5] Liz Alton, "The Evolution From Work-Life Balance to Work-Life Integration," ADP. Last accessed Nov 2, 2021, https://www.adp.com/spark/articles/2018/10/the-evolution-from-work-life-balance-to-work-life-integration.aspx.

[6] "What Success Means to Americans [Infographic]," Strayer University, Last accessed Nov 2, 2021, https://www.strayer.edu/buzz/what-success-means-americans-infographic.

[7] G.E. Miller, "70% of Americans want to be Self-Employed. What is Stopping you?," 20SomethingFinance, Last accessed Nov 2, 2021, https://20somethingfinance.com/self-employment-poll/.

EXERCISE: SUCCESS YOUR WAY

Part I: Current Work-Life Balance

Deep down, the pattern of working hard for success is related to our basic needs of safety and security. Please read through the questions below and circle any scenarios that you recognize in your own life currently.

Do you...

* feel like work is impacting your health?
* feel like you have to make excuses to not participate in social activities because of work?
* want to constantly spend more time on work to get ahead?
* feel like work defines you?
* check messages excessively on weekends, holidays, in the middle of the night, etc.?
* wish that you could balance work and life differently?

Part II: Evaluation of Your Needs

If you answered yes to any of the above, I encourage you to complete the next set of questions and use your journal to write and reflect on your perception of your basic needs.

* What unspoken expectations did your parents have of you?
* What needs were met or not met in childhood?
* What specific situation comes to mind (if any) where you've ignored your needs in the past?
* What specific situation comes to mind (if any) where you are currently ignoring your needs?
* What are your needs today? Are they different from your needs in the past? Notice the difference.

Part III: Redefining Success

Lastly, this last part of the exercise brings us to the definition of success and an opportunity to redefine what success looks and feels like to you. Based on what you have discovered and learned about the connection between your perception of work and your basic needs and any patterns you may notice, please journal about the questions below:

* What is your definition of success currently?
* How do you feel about your current level of life balance?
* What is life balance for you? Describe.
* How can you redefine success for yourself?
* What would be different in your life if you applied your new definition of success?
* What is the first change you will make towards success on your own terms?

2

Pushing Yourself and Ignoring Your Needs

> *"It's not the destination, it's the journey."*
> — Ralph Waldo Emerson

G rowing up, every March we went on a ski trip to northern Sweden. We were fortunate enough to borrow a relative's beautiful log cabin in a desirable ski area for a week. One of the things that I loved about our ski vacation was the adventure of driving far north. The drive was somewhere between eight and ten hours long. As we journeyed across the country, I was watching the landscape change from familiar rural towns to busy, dense cities and eventually reach the beautiful wilderness up north. Usually, we stopped overnight halfway at a small hotel, which was an adventure in itself.

Most of the years we traveled with another family with kids our age and we spent the entire week skiing the familiar slopes. We got up early in the morning, packed ourselves and the gear in the car, and skied until the lifts were closing at four in the afternoon.

I remember taking off the skis, sitting in the snow, turning my face towards the sun, eating the egg sandwiches, and drinking the hot chocolate my mom made to bring for lunch. My eleven-year-old self thought, *I hope this never ends*, and took another bite from my egg sandwich.

On the other hand, the weeks leading up to the departure for the long-awaited trip left a different soul memory in me.

Every year leading up to this treasured week of vacation, I felt anxiety. For weeks before our departure, I watched my mom working herself to exhaustion, preparing taxes for the customers at the bank. The reason she was doing this was to earn enough money so that our family could go on the ski trip.

The massive push and effort put in on my mom's part were palpable, as if this trip was completely dependent on whether she could get all the taxes done on time.

She worked through late nights on top of her full-time job hours, and as a child, I thought it was normal and necessary that my mom had to be so stressed and exhausted, but I felt it too.

Stress and rush were very much present at home at that time, my mom organizing and packing the bags and suitcases and constantly asking questions: "Will it all fit in the car? What if we forgot something?"

The relief and happiness we felt when we *finally* hopped in the car and got on the road were like going over the finish line in a race.

The candy bags were ready to be opened. The magazines were ready to be read. Promises were made between my younger sister and me not to fight while in the car (or the entire trip, for that matter).

And *finally*, my mom could sit down while my dad was driving.

The Void Within

This experience of watching my mom extend herself to the limits of exhaustion left a strong impression on me that "If I want something, I have to put ALL my effort in and push through any obstacle. I have to extend myself to the max, and THEN, if I work hard and do a good job, maybe I can sit down and enjoy myself."

More importantly, I received the message: "Before hitting that desired finish line, it's always a race, and nothing else matters." I thought I was supposed to be a machine that just kept going, ignoring my needs to reach the finish line at all costs. That's the way it was shown to me.

Many of us have witnessed parents ignoring their own emotional and physical needs, living driven by their minds. When a life pattern is demonstrated to us in childhood, it becomes magnified, and a lasting impression is imprinted. For some previous generations, this behavior of pushing through was necessary to simply survive, so the pattern of switching off emotions to continue on is perhaps well ingrained in us all at this point.

When we combine the desire to please with a strong will and belief in scarcity, we can drive ourselves so far away from our own sense of limits without noticing it. We stop listening to our hearts and inner voices so that our minds and logic can take over and problem solve without influence from our emotional needs and boundaries. It's like our inner world of emotion and the connection with our body is silent and non-existent. It's like the silent treatment of oneself.

A few years back, I could work an entire day, multitasking at full speed, and yet still continue a few more hours in the evening when the kids were in bed. My focus on the task at hand was what mattered, ignoring me as a person, living my life that day.

Things just had to be completed. No negotiation was available with me. It was like a switch to my feelings was turned off, and in that neutral place within I could continue as long as it was needed without questioning myself, or asking why, or honoring the inner voice saying, "Time to stop?!"

What happens when we ignore our own needs?

Some call it the void within, where no feelings are present, only mind focus. That empty space within that creates nothing more than a piercing energy projected outwards when completely immersed in the task at hand.

Within that void, we stop the feedback loop between giving and receiving and only project the energy of giving until it's done.

Codependency is a form of ignoring our needs, and it starts in childhood. As children, for various reasons, we had to adapt to the priorities of our parents. These priorities make the child feel like their wants and needs for attention are being ignored and may result in feelings of abandonment. The need to regain attention is still there, and as adults, the pattern continues as we sacrifice our own needs and wants in relationships. Feelings of resentment, emptiness, and blaming others may occur as a result.

It should be mentioned here that our needs are not only emotional. Other needs may be mental, emotional, spiritual, physical, and social needs, as well as needs for autonomy, integrity, and a need for expression.[8,9]

It's easy to ignore the experience of today, and only live in the future. It surely is a multitasking life out there that keeps us from experiencing the moment that is right now.

We often feel exhausted after a long week. We don't have the energy or want to look at what's happening today in our lives; we just want to focus on the future and move on to a better tomorrow.

Some of us keep feeling frustrated and overwhelmed, stuck and just getting through the day. We struggle to move forward, so we procrastinate and worry. We don't want to deal with the relationship issues that have been going on for way too long. The pressure within to figure things out is making us feel lost and even unsafe sometimes.

We don't want to sit down with our today and see it for what it is.

And yet another day goes by.

Stuck as ever.

Without being here today and humbly seeing it for what it is, tomorrow is created out of an illusion based on other people's experience and our ego mind's limited perspective, instead of the true reality as it is now.

A relentless mind focus on work and pushing through to avoid lack of financial security, which, in my case, was one of the main reasons per my childhood values, were evident in all the years of my professional career. Today, I realize that the pattern of getting completely focused on work at the expense of myself and my own needs is not leading to increased security and abundance.

Abundance in the form of financial security, as an example, is an energy that shows up when we are in balance within ourselves and not something we can push ourselves onto. It's an energy flow that's coming to us when we align with the energy of abundance, not necessarily when we work hard.

---

[8] Darlene Lancer, "Meeting Your Needs Is the Key to Happiness," PsychCentral, Last accessed Nov 2, 2021, https://psychcentral.com/lib/meeting-your-needs-is-the-key-to-happiness#1.

[9] Timothy J. Legg, "Codependency: How Emotional Neglect Turns Us into People-Pleasers," Healthline, Last accessed Nov 2, 2021, https://www.healthline.com/health/mental-health/codependency-and-attachment-trauma.

So, my long-held belief that "the harder I work, the safer I'm going to be" didn't stick at all. In fact, later in my adult life, this belief was proven to be detrimental to my soul growth and happiness because for me it closed off some of the most powerful energies we can tap into as human beings. The energies of our passion and creativity. Similarly, the belief that "the more I try to reach for what is regarded as successful (i.e., rewarded with money or promotion), the more successful I become" didn't stick either.

These beliefs showed themselves to be only half-baked strategies in utilizing my true, innate talents and gifts, which are both feminine and masculine qualities, ideally in harmony with each other. Many of the feminine aspects of myself, such as trusting my intuition, spending time in reflection, ability to receive without effort, and awareness of body wisdom and emotional intelligence, were parts of me that had been shut down for so long, to cope and survive under the dominance of the masculine energy quality of the logical mind.

The pattern of pushing myself to the limit, for example, working long hours, the mind-driven, tangible, material focus I had spent so many years maintaining, is the complete *opposite* from the go-with-the-flow, feminine, intuitive, heart connection.

You may be recognizing yourself in some aspect of my example. If you do, now you have a prime opportunity to reconnect to you feminine energy to allow yourself to honor your needs fully by prioritizing your own self-care so that you can experience life balance and harmony.

Exercise:
A Self-Care Practice

Part I: Five Minutes to Bring Yourself Back

It is essential to bring back balance in your life. This exercise begins with a reality check on your current situation. Return to your journal and reflect on how your daily patterns impact your need for self-care and life balance.

Questions to ask yourself:

* In what situations are you pushing through and ignoring your own needs?
* Thinking back, when did you start ignoring your own needs? (This could be different for each need/situation.)
* Reflect on who was/is involved in the situations when you ignore your own needs?
* In what areas of your life would you like to see a change?
* What would be different if you were breaking free from these pattern(s)?

If you are ignoring your needs, it's likely you don't have much time to yourself. If you feel you are in the rat race, I give you permission to step aside today. Self-care is creating space for just yourself in your day.

Try this simple journaling practice:

Take five minutes just with yourself. It may feel very different to just sit down and focus only on you (and not others), but try it.

In your journal write down some words that describe how you feel right now. These words may not be positive; that's fine. Just writing down how you feel right now in this moment is freeing.

Tomorrow, do the same thing. Set a timer and take just five minutes to yourself, with yourself. Notice the space that you are creating for yourself. Reflect on your day so far.

Look out the window. Notice how you feel. Don't feel tempted to answer that email that came into your inbox or pay attention to that laundry beep that you just heard. It can wait.

Change can take many forms, but it always includes time for reflection.

Part II: Putting Yourself in the Center

If you want to go deeper, the next simple but powerful exercise will launch you into expanding your sense of self-love.

Think of something you have been wanting to do but have not yet started.

Now, think about it and say the following statements out loud, completing each of the sentences based on what you have determined you want to do:

* I know enough to take the first step to...
* I'll start and see what I can learn by doing...
* I am good enough to...
* I can take the first step today and I will...

How does it feel to say these sentences? (Did you feel a little spark? A little speck of love for yourself, just by saying it out loud?) What if you could start a daily practice of completing these positive sentences out in order to stop pushing yourself and ignoring your needs and invite more of YOU back into your life?

3
Worrying About What Other's Will Think

> *"Worrying is using your imagination to create something you don't want."*
> — Abraham Hicks

When we had people over at our house as a child, my mom would do her utmost to have the perfect meal served. She made sure the house was cleaned and would have my sister and me show up well dressed. There was clear tension in the air of rushing to get things done before people arrived.

It was demonstrated to me that it was important to have everything planned and thought out in advance, well put together, and ready to go when people arrived.

Many years later, I sat down on a kitchen chair after having helped my young girls with their Halloween costumes. My anxiety rose within me to the point of almost crying. I didn't want people to arrive. In the back of my head, I heard my mom say, "What are others going to think?"

My mind continued, *Are they going to think the food is too cold?* and *Have I cooked enough food?* Nobody would know my inner anguish, but on the inside, it destroyed any chance of me enjoying the party hosted for a bunch of neighbors.

Years later, and through experiences of similar situations, I realized I hadn't challenged the desire for perfection within myself. I hadn't asked myself the important question: "Does this really matter to ME?"

My focus on perfection and people pleasing channeled my energy to focus on the fear of "what others were going to think" and how to make a situation appear as perfect as possible, instead of focusing on enjoying the engagement and interaction with our guests.

And after people had left, I often could feel that I didn't even have a chance to talk with any of our guests at all. I had been spending my time running around, making sure everything looked perfect and that everyone had what they needed.

I spent the time after everyone left cleaning up, putting everything back in order.

Showing Up to Be Validated or to Enjoy?

When we focus on something that we automatically believe is important—something that is absorbed and demonstrated through childhood values and patterns—it can function as a subconscious distraction. It becomes a distraction from experiencing ourselves and others fully in the moment.

When we distract ourselves with something external that we believe is important, such as, in my case, constantly tending to the food, at the party, or repeatedly asking everyone if they have what they need, we don't deal with our social insecurities or fears. Rather, we bypass the true inner experience of the present moment.

In an article titled "Self-Compassion, Stress, and Coping" by Batts, Allen, and Leary, distraction is defined as perceived pleasurable activities to distract oneself from a stressful event to avoid confronting the underlying reasons for a problem.[10]

So the stress we may feel when we are in an uncomfortable situation may be eased by maintaining a familiar pattern that was shown to us in childhood, such as worrying about what others will think. But the problem here is that by doing so we don't offer ourselves

---

[10] A.B. Allen and M. R. Leary, "Self-Compassion, Stress, and Coping," *Social and Personal Psychology Compass* 4, no. 2 (2010):107-118, doi:10.1111/j.1751-9004.2009.00246.x.

any insight about why we're distracting ourselves and we don't give ourselves an opportunity to learn something new about ourselves.

Often, we maintain a pattern of distracting ourselves from the present moment without noticing it. That's why it's extra important to observe what we do automatically; things we've engaged in for years and that we're comfortable with.

The more we recognize and let go of our own self-distraction patterns, including attachment to learned patterns from childhood, the more we can open up to listen and learn about how we *appear to ourselves* in the moment.

We're constantly asking others how we show up, and we often receive, "You look GREAT!" or "That was nice of you. Thank you!", but how often do we believe the compliments we hear from others? Do we ever ask ourselves how we feel about how we show up?

Self-love and self-compassion are important gifts we can give to ourselves to balance all the worrying that the mind engages in about what others think.

When we apply self-compassion, we essentially direct the same loving care, kindness, and compassion towards ourselves that we would towards a loved one should they suffer. The act of self-compassion may be far from what our ancestors, parents, or family members demonstrated to us in childhood, but if we can increase the level of self-compassion in our lives and love ourselves enough to let go of the expectations of how we believe we're supposed to show up (or our opinion of how others need to show up), we will eventually start to show up just to share a moment with others, and that becomes enough, even in our own eyes.

As a result, when our self-love and compassion increase, we decrease our tendency to put up a filter of self-distraction or the need for constant external validation. We just don't need the validation like we once did. As this happens, we can start to invite our experience from a higher consciousness, appreciating what is without wanting it to be different, and we can actually start enjoying ourselves.

Many times we're told that what others think of us is what matters, as if that's how we know we've done something right. Often, we need to be liked and validated by others in the form of compliments.

But does this external validation truly help us get to know who we truly are and what matters to us? We often hear that other people around us are mirroring us in some way, but how do we know if that mirror image matters to us?

Personally, the shift from "What are others are going to think?" to "I am enough just the way I am" has provided me with a new feeling of lightness, curiosity, and freedom instead of the previous closed-in heaviness of anxiety, without the need for validation.

Are you worrying about what people will think? How is it affecting your life?

Exercise:
I Am Enough

Part I: Transform Your Worry

In this exercise, you are invited to transform your worry into compassion.

To begin, identify and observe the situations in which you are worrying about what others will think. Notice how this pattern or worrying currently shows up in your life. Is it at work or school? At family functions? At home?

Use your journal and contemplate the following questions:

* How do you feel about the way you show up in those situations?
* What does your worrying prevent you from doing?
* How would you like to show up instead?
* What can you learn from your current situation?

Part II: Find Self-Compassion

Only you can show yourself that you are enough. Compassion is the antidote to self-judgement and worry. Give yourself the gift of self-compassion with this next part of the exercise.

Start on a new page in your journal and write at the top "I Am Enough." Put your hand on your heart and say out loud "I Am Enough."

* What do you feel when you contemplate the above sentence?
* What do you feel when you say the sentence out loud?
* How can you increase your expression of self-love and self-compassion?
* How can you show others compassion?
* How can enjoy yourself more?

Every time you worry about what others will think, put your hand on your heart and repeat "I Am Enough" to yourself. It is extra powerful if you can watch yourself saying it, for example, in front of a mirror, or record yourself and watch it back.

Notice the inner shift over time as you continue this practice.

4
People Pleasing

> *"People pleasing doesn't allow you to receive."*
> — Abiola Abrams

I looked up at the clock on the wall. It was 8:00 p.m. on a Sunday night, and I could feel the resistance rising within me. I sighed to myself. *I don't really want to do this another week.* But, of course, I saw myself doing it another week, even though I wasn't inspired to attend another week of endless meetings and chasing the next client to become interested.

I felt I was never done, there was always something else, and maybe another closet needed organizing after that. I never ended up paying attention to my own needs; I was paying attention to the next item on the to-do list.

My entire being I knew I wasn't motivated to make another call, or put another project in the queue. But I knew I was going to do it anyway. Because the next week was a new week, and it was Monday tomorrow. I took my eyes off the clock and continued folding the last clothes in the laundry basket.

The security of a twenty-year corporate career kept me marching forward without wavering. Week after week, I drove down the same highway again and again. Security was the only reason I kept going as fast as I did.

The instinct and conditioning of needing security at all costs made me not question the situation or look back, only look forward towards a myriad of objectives and goals that were set for me to achieve. And so I did. With a smile on my face and great collaboration skills.

The responsibility of being a wife and mom with a young family, having a full-time job with business travel, and studying for my MBA at night was overwhelming. No wonder my life was so busy. My hand was constantly up, volunteering my energy and saying "yes" to everything, both at home and at work.

I subconsciously allowed myself to take on more and more, which led me to put myself at the very end of the priority list. I rarely did something only for myself and I relied on my work and family to provide the direction and boundaries I needed in terms of what needed to get done.

It was so easy to slip into a world where everything and everyone else was first. In my mind, there was no time for having fun. The pressures of work and having a young family were my definition of having fun. Don't get me wrong, it has been the greatest joy of all to become a parent and watch my girls experience life and grow up. I wouldn't trade it for anything in the world. However, even though being a parent is one of the most enriching experiences we can have in our lives, for me, it was a feeling of endless love associated with being the *responsible* parent. The weight of this great responsibility of parenthood and overwhelm shut off my permission to have fun and to feel spontaneous joy and passion within *for no reason*.

If someone asked me what I loved to do for fun or what I was passionate about in life, I had no answer. There was no room within me that allowed for getting to those answers within; my personal truths were overshadowed by duty and routine. At the time, I thought I knew what joy and what my passions in life were and how they felt; I didn't.

I did not question the situation or ask myself, "How do I feel [about my job]?"

I guess I knew the answer was going to be "I don't know" or "It's fine; it's good pay" or "It's what I know. What else would I do?"

"I don't know" was a very common answer from me during this time in my life.

Never did I wonder why my actions came from a place of mechanic, automatic energy on repeat instead of from a free-flowing, dynamic, heartfelt, inner buzzing sensation of inspiration or effortless creativity and passion.

Why?

Because I believed that I already knew the answers all too well. My expectations were aligned to what society expected or what others wanted of me, so why ask myself questions that I didn't have an answer to anyway?

In hindsight, I know that the biggest reason for not asking myself the deeper questions was that I didn't allow myself to slow down enough to listen to the answers of what I loved to do for fun or in order to find my passion in life because my pattern of people pleasing had everything and everyone else go first.

The Creative Passion Within

When we let everything and everyone else go first, we people please. According to Merriam-Webster Dictionary, a people pleaser is "a person who has an emotional need to please others often at the expense of his or her own needs or desires."[11]

No wonder I didn't know what my passion in life was or what I did for fun!

As mentioned before, my own definition of having fun and feeling passion for life was attached to the responsibilities of taking care of my young family and securing a successful professional corporate career. In other words, my self-identity was defined as my career and being a parent, not who I uniquely was as a person. I believed that if I just worked as hard as I could, it would be my passion.

In addition, what I didn't realize was that I was putting my definition of passion in someone else's hands. In doing so, someone else could determine my self-worth, depending on whether or not they thought I did a good enough job or not. And in that way, my sense of passion and self-worth could be gone in one second if someone said I didn't do a good job or determined that I wasn't needed anymore.

Our true selves are seeking a feeling of heart-buzzing creative passion within, but we are not able to give this level of passion to ourselves, so we're seeking it outside of us. Some are getting their sense of passion and self-worth from people pleasing. The problem is that when passion is not sourced from within, the source of passion shifts depending on the person it's sought from, so it is not stable.

---

[11] Merriam-Webster.com Dictionary, Merriam-Webster, Last accessed Nov 2, 2021, https://www.merriam-webster.com/dictionary/people%20pleaser.

According to an article on WebMD, a people pleaser can be someone who is agreeing with whatever is said, taking on the blame for something that is not their fault, taking on too much and not being able to say no, or taking on opinions or attitudes based on the environment or a person or group and is in need of validation to feel self-worth.[12]

Conditional passion can show itself as a nice compliment, a pat on the back, public recognition, and so on. We feel good because it was given to us in return for our openness and willingness to not question. (Because if we do, we may get judged!) We want the validation to know we're good enough. And if we people please, for example, by adopting someone else's agenda, or when taking someone's advice at face value, or agreeing to someone else's solutions, even if we know it's not right for us, we receive someone else's passion and absorb it.

When we people please and source our ability to feel passion in life from somewhere else, our true selves are left out in the cold.

Many of us were taught to relate through conditional passion. How often growing up did you hear, "If you do well in school and get good grades, you'll…"? For decades, it has been asked of us to show that we can excel within the defined framework of reward for all in the form of grades, degrees, and so on.

When our passion is conditional, expectations of happiness are placed in a defined box with a label on it, and that box is pulled out on the day you graduate or a promotion is announced. It's on those expected occasions when we're supposed to smile and celebrate that we experience conditional passion, and even the happiness that we're emitting may be just a people-pleasing response to uphold an outer image of happiness for others' comfort and approval.

When we completely shift our energy away from our inner experience to focus on an experience of external matters—such as getting good grades, excelling at work, or focusing entirely on our families—and we don't maintain an inner feedback loop of own reflection—we lose the connection to our true self and the inner life force that makes up our true experience of passion in life.

---

[12] WebMD Medical Reference, "What Is a People Pleaser?," WebMD, Last accessed Nov 2, 2021, https://www.webmd.com/mental-health/what-is-a-people-pleaser

During those years of my life when I found myself emotionally neutral and on autopilot, there was no sensation of passion, expansion, creativity, adventure, or exploration of my inner experience.

There was no self-reflection, no curiosity about life, and I didn't ask myself how I could live my life differently, with a different experience as a result.

The idea of having fun was the yearly birthdays celebrated, the summer vacations, the milestones achieved by the girls as they grew up, the celebrated promotions and degree achievements recognized. The feeling of enjoyment was present but without the "life-force bursting passion" element. I call it planned and predictable fun.

Don't get me wrong, I truly enjoyed all of these milestones, but what was missing was that there were no bursts of joy *for no particular reason* at that time in my life.

I realized that what I had experienced in the past was not passion in its fullest expression. The reason I call it conditional passion is because I didn't include *myself* and my needs in the passion part. I only included my career and what I accomplished in my definition of passion.

The difference now is that the passion and joy I know now that is present in my life daily is not dependent on anyone else or what I do. It's the experience of the universal power that we all can connect to and that embraces us unconditionally. This feeling of passion and joy is not connected to what we produce or accomplish. It's unlimited, and there are no conditions.

It's the feeling of unlimited passion when I am in my element, aligned with my own natural energy, and when I'm in balance, authentically expressing my gifts and talents effortlessly.

As previously mentioned, if your source of passion in life is directed towards something outside yourself, for example, a career or a relationship, passion becomes conditional. But when this passion is directed towards the self, it becomes unconditional self-love.

With that transformation comes a change in your inner conversation as well. Our inner voice changes to a softer, more forgiving, and ever-present voice when we feel that passion for no reason and inner life-force bubbling up within us.

We're no longer chasing passion as if it is a moving target. The inner passion of self-love is present within you, and it's permanent.

When self-love is present, there is no need to people please.

Exercise: People Pleasing No More!

In this exercise, you'll identify whether you have the pattern of people pleasing. Below are a few indicators of people-pleasing. Please read through and circle any scenarios that you recognize in your own life.

Part I: The Pattern

When you interact with others at work (or in life), do you:

* feel like you are compromising your inner confidence and desires to satisfy someone else's opinion?
* have to carefully select your words to make sure they are coming out "right"?
* want a positive reaction from the person you are talking to?
* feel like you give more energy out than receive?
* feel resistance to saying no?

If you answer yes to any of the above, you may want to consider the next part of this exercise.

Part II: The Cost

Take out a piece of paper and write down your answers to the questions below:

* What drives your people-pleasing behavior?
* What does this behavior of people pleasing cost you in terms of personal satisfaction and fulfillment?
* In what relationships do you feel you are people pleasing the most? Why?
* What are you really telling yourself on the inside in those situations?

These answers may be difficult to pinpoint, but the more you start observing your own behavior, the more you'll learn about yourself.

With a growing focus on observing yourself and your inner thoughts, you'll grow your own awareness and opportunity to make a change.

How do you know you're no longer people pleasing?

Look for this:

* In interactions with others, you'll start to feel that it's your true self that is speaking, not what you think others want to hear.
* Being able to give someone a "No" without feeling guilty.
* Keeping your energy for yourself instead of giving it away.
* Gaining self-awareness, confidence, and balance in your life and career.

5

Driven by the Ego

> *"It's not your job to like me, it's mine!"*
> — Byron Katie

Years ago, as a young adult, I was going to bring my new boyfriend to an extended family dinner for the first time. We were getting ready, and my boyfriend had changed into something he thought would be suitable to wear for the occasion.

However, I didn't think it was suitable to wear, so I flew off the handle and said, "I don't think you should wear that! Put something better on!!"

He looked at me and obediently turned around without saying a word. I walked him to the closet, knowing the *exact* shirt that I wanted him to wear. I went through his shirts and found it. "Wear this. I like this one much better!"

He quietly said, "OK," turned around, and went to change his shirt without arguing.

I put pride in a strong sense of righteousness. I had to be right, in control, and I was determined to have the last word, judging others to feel better about myself. I was totally unaware of a life lesson that was playing out in full action right in front of me through my strong-headed ego fueled by my low self-esteem.

Unaware and continuing into adulthood, I used to generously offer my best friends opinions and solutions unsolicited. This righteousness was sourced solely from my ego. If someone came to ask me for advice, I knew the answer even before they had finished the question. I thought I did someone a service.

The Voice of the Ego

Before I first discovered that there is something called the voice of the ego, I used to get frustrated and automatically react emotionally in the moment to whatever happened. I allowed situations to take charge of my energy.

In addition, I didn't understand what an inner conversation was, and I didn't know that I could actually learn how to listen to that inner conversation. My perception of myself was: "I'm just the way I am, and I feel the way I feel." Basically, I believed what I was thinking and that I couldn't change what I was thinking. This belief is common of someone that identifies only with their ego.

The ego is defined as our sense of personal identity or feelings of self-importance.[13] Our ego's job is to feel important, and the ego does not live in the present.

Only the present moment truly exists, but our egos want us to think about the past and future, which exist exclusively in our minds. That's why we sometimes refer to the ego as the ego mind. The ego mind just wants to keep our mind distracted, preventing us from fully engaging in our world around us and tuning in to the present moment. It's only in the present moment that we can choose to change something, even our thoughts.

Through training as a life coach, I learned how to identify the ego's voice and listen to it and its stories in a detached manner. In my own experience, my ego's voice was the most active in my day-to-day life, at work, with the kids, and so on, so I had to start observing myself pretty much all the time.

A daily meditation and intuitive journaling practice helped me deepen the skill required to observe myself and my inner conversation. Later on, I learned how to detect and listen to my ego's voice in the moment outside a meditative state in day-to-day life, and that was a game changer, as I now could decide in the moment if I wanted to listen to the ego's chatter or not.

Furthermore, I soon discovered that there was a conversation going on within me that wasn't that supportive at all. I disliked the

---

[13] Alan Watts, "How Your Ego Is Affecting Your Mental Health," iHASCO, Last accessed Nov 2, 2021, https://www.ihasco.co.uk/blog/entry/2206/get-to-know-your-ego.

conversation so much that I didn't want to be part of it. It was a major discovery for me that the chatter that went on in my mind was not my authentic, true self; it was my ego. This insight of noticing the [lack of] quality of the ego's conversation is often what starts someone's transformation to seeking the intentional presence and expansion of their true self's voice more and more in their lives.

All too often we're too emotionally caught up in the situation to be able to objectively observe the dynamic and catch the essence of the lesson. Instead, we become defensive, as the ego does everything it can to maintain the status quo, and continue with the same blame game, widening the unhealed wound and with no change in sight.

Have you ever heard someone say, "It's HER fault that I feel so overwhelmed! She is so rude, and that makes this environment toxic!"? This comment is an example of someone who's in their ego, going right to blame someone else for a situation, instead of wondering how they themselves contributed to it.

The more faults and blame the ego can dig up, the more we struggle. When we are in the energy of finding the faults of others or when we feel that others are the reason we struggle, it's showing us where our wounds are within ourselves.

It's like it's the ego's job is to amplify and point out where we need to heal. When we complain about something, whether it's a relationship or a situation at home or work, this is an indication that it may be the *exact* dynamic we need to heal within ourselves.

Interestingly, if we were to listen to ourselves in those situations where we struggle, we could easily pick up a clue from what's going on. The opportunity is to translate that clue into what it is that we need to heal and learn from it if we want to.

Personally, my ego's voice did everything it could to defend my disciplined work schedule and level of commitment to my career, even when I realized that it wasn't what I truly wanted. I wasn't listening to the numerous clues that I was given.

As I was struggling with a heavy workload and business travel, I simply missed the clues that I needed more flexibility in my workday and fewer items in my schedule to thrive.

As I struggled with fulfilling my to-do list every day, I missed the clues about giving room for more creativity, bringing forward my inner voice, and unlocking my spiritual gifts and the connection with the Universe.

As I was struggling to multitask at home and getting frustrated with the kids, pushing myself to exhaustion, I missed the clues that I needed to come to terms with negotiating away my need for self-care, needed to learn how to prioritize and make space for myself in my life, and needed to love myself first.

As I was struggling with my conditioned desire to plan, organize, and control to fulfill an expected picture of perfect happiness, I missed the clues that I needed to loosen the grip, let go of my career, reinvent myself, and invite ease and flow to connect to my life's purpose. The list goes on…

What made me stop midair was that day when I received that surprising phone call and the Universe said, "ENOUGH!!!" That day I simply was served with an opportunity to choose. To listen or to not listen.

Clearly, this experience of losing my job was carefully orchestrated by the Universe to hit at the deepest level of my soul. It was a much-needed life lesson that was served to me on a silver platter for me to experience and go through. It was tailored to hit just right. To wake me up.

Luckily, I chose to listen and learn from the ego's screaming voice and to become aware of what was really going on to learn what I needed to heal within.

Once I could identify the ego's voice, it was time to let go of the part of me that wanted me to stay where I was, especially concerning my career. Instead, I intentionally began to invite more airtime for my true self's voice to step forward to help guide me on my life's path.

What I needed to transform and heal to become a happier me became so transparent. I needed to learn to trust in a completely new way and not trust my limited ego mind perspective, which always needed evidence of worthiness. Instead, I needed to trust myself and what I could not see as an expanded and much more powerful being, which is the expression of my true self.

In the end, I promised myself that I would never allow my ego to attach my self-worth to a job (or anything else) ever again.

So many people with huge egos and lack of self-awareness have crossed my path, blaming everything but themselves for their situations. These people had to cross my path because I personally had to learn to not play into or emotionally engage in situations of tension or dramas between people and instead learn how to detach from taking things personally.

Also, with the experience of being around people with huge egos, I was given an opportunity to reflect on how my ego mind plays out. When I started to believe that people show up in my life to teach me something, my focus completely changed.

The ego mind thrives on valuing what we can see with our own eyes. This is because the ego mind believes that the only things that are real are the things we can see. Most importantly, the ego mind wants us to stay in the past or continue to figure out the future—and only in its own way! Our egos will stomp around in our unhealed wounds, making them louder, sharper, and deeper until we decide to stop and listen.

Personally, I had to transform into someone who aligns and co-creates with universal energy as part of a higher purpose. I needed to transform the energy of co-dependency and lack of self-worth to learn how to receive self-love in a completely new way. I had to learn that love that is unconditional comes from just being, and conditional love, the "traditional" love as we know it, is based on giving and expecting something in return. I had to step into a new level of self-empowerment and an authentic self-expression based on my true self.

How about you? What will you do?

Our ego mind doesn't have all the answers.

What we see is not all there is.

There is MORE...

Exercise:
Listen to Your Inner Conversation

In this exercise you'll spend time listening to your ego's conversation by observing yourself. Pick a time during your day, set a timer for 10 minutes, and focus on noticing your thoughts as you continue with what you're doing on a normal day. As you catch a thought, write it down.

(Hint! Even as you read this exercise, there is a conversation going on within you that you may or may not notice.)

After the 10 minutes of observation and listening, sit down and read through your notes.

What did you notice about your ego's voice during the 10 minutes? For example, did it use a specific tone or words or make assumptions or interpretations?

Then contemplate the following questions:

* Who in your life is leading with their ego? What can you learn from them?
* What do you avoid feeling or doing by listening to the ego mind's chatter?
* How would you like your inner conversation to be instead?

The way you're going to separate the ego's voice from your true self's voice is by carefully listening and sensing what your truth is. The ego's voice is often judgmental and is relating to the situation by drawing from the past or desiring something different (in the future). Notice if you can separate the voice of the ego versus your true self based on your notes. If not right away, that is fine too. It takes practice.

PART 2
Heart-Centered Living: The Fundamentals

"What lies before us and what lies behind us
Are small matters
Compared to what lies within us.
And when you bring
What is within out into the world
Miracles happen."

— Henry David Thoreau

To live from the heart and intuition is to live in harmony with the present moment. With this comes the opportunity to expand ourselves and break free from our routine lives, ingrained patterns, and struggles and to live life away from the mind's limiting beliefs.

It's an experience of life that is already available to us if we decide to tap into it. It's an experience of truth and expansion as we activate a connection that is greater than our physical self. In Part 2, you'll get familiar with the six key elements of heart-centered living that contribute to an expanded consciousness, a deepened trust in yourself, and a connection with wisdom beyond what you know.

1. Energy Awareness

I believe that becoming aware of our energy is as essential in our life as learning how to read. The experience of life never becomes dull when we connect with our energy body and different dimensions of life than just the physical plane. In Chapter 6, energy awareness is discussed as a path to self-empowerment, and you will learn how you can stop giving your energy away.

2. Creativity and Inspiration

The ability to expand and perceive things beyond what is seen with our eyes is supported by our ability to visualize and dream. And it starts with tapping into our creativity and inspiration. When we live from the heart, we are motivated from within by our true selves. In Chapter 7, you'll explore setting intentions and dream BIG!

3. Intuition and Inner Knowing

Everyone has intuitive abilities of some kind. As we learn how to listen to our intuition, we expand to trust our inner voice and our truth. We can also connect with our spirit guides, which are always communicating with us. In Chapter 8, you'll practice listening to your inner truth through intuitive journaling.

4. Nature Connection

Ease and flow are found in nature's cycles. The more we intentionally align with the effortless ease and flow already existing in nature, the more we experience harmony and balance in our lives. In Chapter 9, you'll experience the impact of tuning into the awe and power of nature.

5. The Body's Wisdom

There's wisdom beyond what our minds can figure out. The body is our vessel to experience an expanded dimension of life. By intentionally tuning in to the body's wisdom, we can notice the messages it has for us. In Chapter 10, you'll experience special messages from your body.

6. Signs and Synchronicities

Heart-centered living is a way to shift our perception and live in direct contact with the miracles we are presented with every day. The language with which the Universe is guiding us forward on our life path is through intuitive downloads, signs, and synchronicities. In Chapter 11, you'll tap into the wisdom of the Universe given to you in the form of signs.

6

Energy Awareness

> *"If you want to find the secrets of the universe,*
> *think in terms of energy, frequency and vibration."*
> — Nicola Tesla

I made a quick stop at a local store on the way home from work. Immediately, when I entered the store, I smelled the fresh aroma of citrus. My eyes came across a frame with the quote by the Chinese philosopher Lao Tzu: "Nature does not hurry. Yet everything is accomplished." I picked up the frame and held it up.

This quote revealed a hidden truth for me. There was something within me in that moment that connected the dots about what really makes things happen. It probably stirred an ancient memory within me about how things are put into form naturally as shown in nature by the primal energies of manifestation and divine timing.

Here I was, spending my day rushing around and now hurrying home, trying to keep that gas pedal down to keep the speed up in my life as much as possible. I had a constant feeling of pressure to be everywhere and do everything at the same time, not only physically but also mentally. I thought I was quite skilled in multitasking at the time and took pride in it.

But as I processed the essence of the citrus in the air and this quote of truth expressed through the words by Lao Tzu, it struck my heart in a completely new way. The quote brought me a peaceful feeling of complete contentment, almost as if I was sitting still on a beach, watching the sunrise; watching the rebirth of a new day. All according to divine plan and natural forces.

What I felt reading this quote was this effortless coming together of myself and the environment, and I realized that "THIS is what I want!" The accomplishment without the hurry! I had no idea this could be a thing! I thought it was absolutely brilliant!

A complete shift was initiated within me that day in the local store. An idea was born within me that awoke a willingness to search for more balance and harmony in my life under the assumption that I could still accomplish what I wanted to do and yet exist in peace.

As I walked out of the store with my framed quote carefully wrapped in tissue paper, still with a peaceful vision of the sun rising before me, I knew I had discovered something essential for my own personal growth.

I had been shown the opportunity to shift my beliefs around how to apply my energy to accomplish things. With this I was also given an opportunity to decide to see things differently.

As I unwrapped my precious frame and put it front and center on my desk, this key insight about my own energy and the energy of everything around us made me start to reevaluate the hustle mentality. I also started to question if multitasking all day long and spreading myself too thin was the best way for me to accomplish something when I wanted it.

In addition, I started to feel the need to return to nature as a source to align with the energy of balance and natural flow, inspired by this quote.

It inspired me to make daily decisions to spend time outside more often. I could feel my energy recharging just by spending time close to a tree or water. I realized that I didn't have to do anything; it just happened. And that was a completely new experience for me. Imagine that—not having to DO anything!

I noticed that if I intentionally spent time interacting with nature, like noticing a flower or observing an insect, I always came back refreshed—physically, mentally, emotionally, and spiritually.

I spent time noticing the intricate details of a tree leaf, or tree bark, or letting my eyes follow a wave or stream, not just walking by it and thinking about something else.

After tuning in to how I felt, I noticed that anytime I was standing still in front of a tree, I felt contentment as if the tree's peaceful and wise energy was shared with me.

Learning about Your Energy

How does your own energy show up in your daily life? The connection between the physical and the phenomenon of energy is a well-researched topic in the world of quantum physics, and the Earth's dynamics and the physical body are core to many of the healing arts and the topic of energy medicine. We are made up of energy, and the environment around us is made up of energy. Yet the concept of energy may be quite abstract to many.

When we become aware of our energy and learn ways to stay in high-energy frequency, we can begin to experience life differently from before. When we start being curious about what makes up our natural flow of energy, we can turn that insight into, for example, how our energy can support us instead of draining us.

To learn how we can set our own energy boundaries that help make daily interactions with others less overwhelming, and we may start to say no more often to give ourselves more time to contemplate and recharge. The idea here is to begin to notice our energy on a daily basis.

By becoming aware of our energy, we can align with the natural flow of the energy of nature and we can learn how to direct and utilize energy to support us. By becoming energy aware and raising our frequency, we can align to higher Universal frequency and wisdom and expand our perspective beyond the mind-driven patterns and beliefs that may keep us stuck.

Are you wondering, *How do I know what my energy is?* or *How can I raise my vibration?* Simplified, often our energy frequency is defined as the level we vibrate emotionally. According to Dr. David R. Hawkins' Map of Consciousness (TM), enlightenment has the highest frequency of over 700 Hz and the greatest expansion of energy. The vibrational frequency of joy is 540 Hz and is expansive. The vibrational frequency of anger is 150 Hz.[14] So, by first noticing our emotions and then reaching for an emotion higher on the scale than what the emotion you're feeling currently, you raise your vibration.

Our energy body is much bigger than we think. The energy body is enveloped by our aura. According to Collins Dictionary, "An aura is a quality or feeling that seems to surround a person or place or to come from them."[15]

---

[14] David R. Hawkins, "Map of Consciousness®," Veritas Publishing, https://veritaspub.com/product/map-of-consciousness-dr-david-hawkins/.
[15] COBUILD Advanced English Dictionary, HarperCollins Publishers, Last accessed Nov 2, 2021, https://www.collinsdictionary.com/us/dictionary/english/aura.

The anatomy of the energy body includes energy channels and energy centers. Each subtle energy body connects to the physical body through energy centers called chakras. There are hundreds of chakras in the energy anatomy, and seven chakras that are most known. The four energy bodies are mental, emotional, physical, and the spiritual.[16]

With our aura we also create energetic connections beyond the human body to everything around us, including the energy of the Universe and existing Earth energies. Our aura reflects our state of energy frequency and well-being to others. Some individuals are gifted with being able to see auras around people through color. Different colors have different energy frequencies.

We don't have to see aura with our own eyes to sense someone's energy body, though. Most of the time we sense someone's energy body through our energy body. If someone is happy, we can sense it, even if we're blindfolded, and if someone is sad, we can sense it too, without looking at the person.

Have you sensed someone's aura before? We often sense the aura through our emotions.

My client Ashley came to me because she didn't feel connected to her life and she wanted to feel more openness, awaken her passion, and let go of her need to control. When we talked about what she wanted, she said, "I just don't know." It turned out that she had a fear of failure, overthinking her actions, and the thought of "What if I'm wrong?" plagued her. She was an empath, sensitive to others' energies, and had closed off her senses and abilities to believe in herself. After working together for three months, her true self emerged. She truly has a rebel nature that had been shut down early in life and by her own sensitive reactions. She wrote to me: "The week has been great. Feeling in the groove. I started noticing that I'm feeling more, which is exciting. I have been thinking a lot about how I don't have to fit in a box—the ideas of who I am supposed to be or how I am supposed to act in society's views. I feel like that is my inner rebel showing herself more."

We worked to awaken her natural abilities to sense others' energy. If she previously was weary of walking into work, not knowing what energy would meet her, we worked on her tuning into the energy BEFORE she went to work so that she could have a sense of it before

---

[16] "What Is the Energy Body?," Just Be Well, Last accessed Nov 2, 2021, https://justbewell.info/what-is-the-energy-body/.

she entered the building. We also worked on energetic boundaries so that she wouldn't give her energy away during the workday and would be able to handle others' energy in a different way.

We may feel good around someone who is in the frequency of compassion rather than someone who is angry. When we share our aura with others, we may take on someone else's energy, and vice versa. This can lead to what is called entanglement as described by quantum physics theories of subatomic particles, leading some scientists to believe our own energy particles may get "entangled" with other people's, especially family and close relationships.

If you've ever felt drained or exhausted after being with someone who was complaining or dumping their emotional baggage on you in an hour-long monologue, you have not only given your energy away but also a case of entanglement has likely occurred.

Part of self-empowerment through energy awareness is to first become aware of our energy body and then realize that we don't have to give our energy away if we don't want to, without having to change a situation or anyone in return.

For me, it has changed the definition of creativity in such a way that creativity no longer stops with something tangible, like something we draw on a piece of paper or words on a page that becomes a book that others can read. Creativity is so much more than that and is a way to connect and expand our energy awareness and connect with our deepest inner talents and gifts.

With our awareness of our energy body, we can link creativity to heart energy and the energy of intuition, which are gateways to pure creativity as facilitated by the Universe.

As Lao Tzu's powerful quote spoke to me in that moment in the local store, I connected with the interdependence and flow between the energy body, the limitless cosmic universal energies, and the earthly energy environment that takes creation and our role in it to a whole new level.

As you learn about your energy body, and you start to see that energy is within us and around us at all times, you may also expand your own definition and view on creativity. The realization that your energy body is not separate from your environment or anyone else in it may make the importance of creativity so much more profound in your life.

Exercise: Exploring Energy

Part I: Basic Energy Awareness

If you've never explored the concept of energy before, start with holding your hands parallel with each other. Imagine that there's a ball of invisible energy between your hands. After a while, you'll start to feel this ball. THAT'S ENERGY!

Another way to relate to energy is to notice the energy between yourself and another person. Stand at an arm's length from them, and notice their energy. Just try it! Just by intentionally noticing, you'll sense the other person's energy, and they will notice yours.

Part II: Intentional Energy Awareness

One way to be intentional about energy is to practice noticing your energy shifting or being impacted when you're around different people or situations.

* Which people or situations in your life do you feel good being around?
* Which people or situations do you **not** feel good being around?

Reflect on why there may be a difference based on your observations.

Another way to be intentional about energy is to set an intention to keep your energy to yourself during the day in every interaction. Before you walk into a place, it could be anywhere, sense the energy before you enter and set an intention for how you want to experience your day.

Reflect on the difference between when you do this and not do this.

Part III: Stop Giving Your Energy Away

When you hold on to an emotion rather than letting it flow through you, you give your energy away. This often happens when we're attached to the outcome of a situation. Examples include:

* worrying over why something is not happening that you really want to happen.
* being upset about not achieving a goal you had set up in the exact time you had planned.
* complaining about someone who is driving you up the wall.

Part IV: Practice Appreciation

Connection to your true self in the situations presented in Part III of this exercise means that you don't dwell on it. For example, when things are not happening the way you want, you can keep your energy intact by letting the emotion flow through you. Then, you let go of the expectation by affirming: "It didn't happen, so it wasn't for me right now" and practice appreciation.

Here are a few simple ways to practice appreciation:

* Take out your favorite journal and write down all your desires and wants, then read them out loud for 30 days in a row and add this sentence: "I am giving [whatever your desire is] away. I'm letting it go."
* Every day, write and say out loud: "Today I'm grateful for [write and say what you're grateful for]." These don't have to be big things in life. Challenge yourself to write down little things that exist in your physical world that surrounds you, as well as things from your inner mental, emotional, and spiritual world.
* Notice what you put down. Are there mostly external or internal things about your life that you appreciate? Why do you think that is?

7
Creativity and Inspiration

> *"Let inspiration lead you wherever it wants to lead you."*
> — Elizabeth Gilbert

This day was special. I had signed up for a workshop for creatives. *What? Me? A creative workshop? No way!* But something told me to sign up for this workshop, so there I was.

There were several things we needed for this workshop—canvases, paint, fabric, ribbons, confetti, etc. Things that I hadn't owned in a long time, or ever...

I was filled with anticipation for the day. I had no idea what was going to happen, but my soul had brought me here, and I was willing to experience something new to expand my soul.

I logged on to the first session. It was a drumming session where we were supposed to get into the rhythm of creativity. It was awesome! I got so engaged that my whole body was swaying, and I felt like I was somewhere else as we sat on the floor together virtually.

The feeling of being one with my body and fully engaged in something was such a freeing feeling after all the years of always being on my way to the next thing, wanting to be somewhere else.

At this moment, I was just there in the present.

Next, we pulled out the canvases and some paint. The drumming continued. I picked up my brush, hesitating for a second. Then, I heard the drumming, and the seductive sound spoke directly to my body. The hesitation disappeared.

The paint came onto the canvas in splotches and strikes—a vivid pattern that I'd never seen before. The drumming got quieter for a moment.

We were encouraged to close our eyes and tap into our deepest desires. We were asked to declare what we wanted next and put it right on the canvas. "Wow!" I heard my inner voice say. "I am a gifted, abundant spiritual teacher, coach, and guide."

Uhm! What? My mind brought me out of the flow for a second. *What did you say?!*

The sentence was repeated to me again, and I felt a warmth inside. I looked for the black color, dipped the brush in the paint, and started to write the exact sentence I just heard.

The workshop host asked us to continue and finish up the painting. I added a few more colors and finished it off with some embellishments. I could no longer see the sentence I put on the canvas.

But I could feel it.

I could imagine it.

I could dream it.

I could believe it.

Soul Creativity

How long time can you go without being truly inspired? One of the biggest lessons I have learned is that if I'm not inspired every day, I'm not bringing out my talents and gifts and I'm not living my true potential.

Inspiration through imagination is the fuel to step into your confidence. The energy of confidence and expansion doesn't pair with the energy of stress; they are of two different frequencies.

So, how can you stay inspired? Imagine you giving yourself the space you need to not let yourself get drained.

The saying, "If we can dream it and believe it, we can create it" has been used many times when it comes to encouraging people to manifest their dreams. But here's the thing—many of us go directly to the "create it" phase without tapping into the "dream it" and "believe it" phases first, and that may be due to our culture of wanting to have things done right away and the need to push and rush to make it happen.

For too long, people have been disconnected from their natural ability to create, and some don't believe that they are creative at all because it is not tangible; the human eye can't see it or the progress in an instant.

Often, I work with clients that don't believe that they can dream up and create something novel in their lives. They don't trust that they're able to create exactly what they want

Do you feel you're creative? Do you see creative opportunities in your daily life that could help you stay inspired and feel good?

Our natural state is being creative, but the ego often wants us to stay where we are. And with a society and social culture that has thrived on rules and regulations, we have slowly defaulted to predetermined scenarios. Creativity has been tucked away to only a few and is not regarded as a natural way of living.

Some of us have even been tempted to take a shortcut to creation by looking over our shoulders to take a sneak peek at what others have already created. Sorry to say, but that's not creation; that's copying.

Copying is one of our ego's best strategies because it's quick and it allows us to move on to the next thing. I believe that why so many of us are choosing the shortcut to copy parts or the whole of other people's creations, either unconsciously or intentionally; what is already created is something that we can see with our own eyes, and therefore, it's easier to believe in.

However, when we're talking about creativity, we're referring to the ability to stretch beyond what is known or seen and truly reconnect with the Universe and our innate talents. Everyone is creative if we allow ourselves to be in the energy of possibility.

As we turn more and more to focus on our inner journey (as opposed to everything external), we are encouraged to go deeper into expanding our dreams and envision and what we believe is possible beyond what is currently in physical form. We are encouraged to go into visualization; to dream, envision, and believe in the creation from within first. To think big and expand beyond what is seen requires tapping into our inner truth and what we *truly* are passionate about. And if we can bring ourselves to truly dream, envision, and believe in co-creation with the Universe, to uncover what our true self is calling us to create, our reality will manifest in completely new ways that have never been experienced before.

No longer is creativity just a "thing" that we produce to put out there for others to admire. I believe that the energy of creativity is now becoming a way to live in harmony with the infinite moment. Creativity becomes a way to intentionally connect, align ourselves with the Universe, and live in balance where literally anything is possible.

We can expand beyond what we used to believe is possible. The thoughts and beliefs that are sourced from our true selves through our intuition and heart energy are pure creativity — the energy and seeds of creation.

As one of my clients, Emily, so beautifully put it in her journal following a coaching session: "I think to be happy, to stop and smell the roses, and to have emotional well-being in an organized fashion, is all actually the same rolled all into one. As I dive into this trinity of energy, I feel I have unlocked parts of myself that I didn't know were locked up. I didn't realize, until now, that to be happy means to explore myself fully. To live, create, and express my life as me. I didn't do that before to this extent because I didn't know who I was like I thought I did. To unlock and discover what's inside me. To transform energies from unhelpful to helpful. To lean into myself, learn about myself, and to get to know myself at a very deep level. To live uniquely as me, show up as me, move through the world as me, to communicate as me now that I'm getting much better at it. To continue to unlock each room inside of me that is dusty and dark. I have recently revealed that there's an abundance of treasure inside."

This creative energy is sourced at the soul level, not at the ego level, and can be described as pure creativity. Pure creativity is life force energy, and even if it's going against what makes sense logically to the mind and what our previous experience is, it makes us unstoppable.

EXERCISE:
Inspired Imagination and
Dreaming Big!

This exercise was designed to spark your inspiration and encourage you to incorporate creativity into your daily life.

What inspires you today?

1. Put on your favorite calming, inspiring song. Close your eyes and take a slow, full, deep breath in through your nose and out through your mouth.
2. Visualize your life as a big-picture view of your situation just as you would like it to be; a life you want to create for yourself. See yourself having FUN! How do you feel? See your face smiling. Be brave and take a look at what this image tells you!
3. Visualize a picture of yourself in this ideal situation and environment. Are there any smells and sounds? Envision the details in your environment. How do you feel in your body? What are you wearing?
4. Add in others close to you into this context (this never fails to inspire and give you even more perspective). Who are you with?
5. What is it about this vision that REALLY excites you? Skip the circumstances and limitations for a moment and go for it! Don't stop until you have a smile on your face and that bubbly feeling in your body. Sit with this vision for at least five minutes.
6. Now open your eyes and take five minutes to write down what you visualized. Don't stop to edit anything. Keep the music going until you are finished.

If you want to take this even further, you can make this visualization into an art project and create something to embody this vision. It could be painting, clay, or any other form that you'd create with your hands.

The important part is to stretch yourself beyond what you think is possible and let go of the judgments and limitations.

Let yourself be in the moment. Catch the sparks of inspiration that come up as a surprise. That's the gold!

8
Intuition and Inner Knowing

> *"Intuition doesn't tell you what you want to hear;
> it tells you what you need to hear."*
> — Sonia Choquette

I looked out the window from my office. It was cloudy and rainy. I hadn't been outside much lately, and I felt stressed and worried. *Why am I not farther along with my project?* My raced. *I should be way ahead by now, but I'm not.*

I had so many thoughts running through my mind, but I didn't know what direction to take this project in.

I asked myself, over and over again, *What is the answer?*

Immediately my mind said, *I have no idea… Maybe there are other options.*

The restlessness I felt inside was unbearable. *This HAS to come together. Otherwise, I'm toast!*

Still looking outside, the clouds seemed to separate quickly, and the sun was about to come out. I felt the urge to go outside. The sun was calling me to come join the magic out there, which would help me to feel alive again.

Immediately, I noticed a tall tree outside that seem to say to me: "Come on! Come outside and play!"

So, what am I doing inside? I asked myself. *Why am I not joining this magic outside?*

I stepped into my backyard with my eyes steady on the tree that had beckoned me. I took a deep breath to smell the rain that just had stopped, the grass still wet from getting a nice shower.

Fresh moist air hit my lungs as I took a deep breath. Now putting my hand on the tree trunk, I could smell its bark.

Suddenly, a distinct feeling rose within me: "I know the answer to the question I was struggling with!"

A spark of inspiration!

A burst of creativity just showed up from nowhere!

I reached for my phone in my back pocket and hurried to bring up a blank page. My inner voice just shared the most brilliant idea. I didn't want to lose this idea so I typed it down quickly. Then, it was gone. It was a gift for stepping out and into the magic for a moment.

I looked up, smiled at the tree, and said, "Thank you!"

Answer delivered!

I gave the tree a big hug while saying to myself, "I have to go outside more often!"

When It's Time to Play

Do you negotiate with yourself, back and forth, worrying, *Should I do this, or should I do that?* And your mind is flip-flopping on every option. *I don't know what's best* or *Let me check a few more things first.* Does this sound familiar?

Often, when we're living our life by the mind, we're driven by worry, anxiety, self-centeredness, and what we don't have in our life. It's evident that all we hear are the mind's limiting beliefs, which makes us feel stuck and small.

When we live a life driven by the mind, we're not connected to the wisdom and truth of our true selves. When we're sitting there at our desks, hour after hour, in our perceived world of progress, we're in a comfortable, cookie-cutter world of expectations where we don't have to use any truly unique, creative ways of solving things.

It's time for us to go outside, awaken, play, and connect with the most intuitive of all, which is nature. Immerse ourselves in nature and align with the natural creation of it all, instead of pushing to make solutions to show up in the ways we want them to.

Instead, we're expected to use our acquired learned skills and be measured against some five-step rating scale on a yearly basis with little flexibility. We just have to do what is expected. And if we do what is perceived to be successful, we've "made it."

When we live a life driven by the mind, we don't have to connect and listen to those sparks of inspiration or our inner voice to take a step out of the ordinary. But when our inner voice, facilitated by our intuition, gets a word, the mind game is over, and we start to listen from within. The feeling of expansion and possibility is overwhelmingly present as we tune into our inner voice and truly listen.

The connection between our intuition, our body, and the energy flow of Earth is undeniable. The constant creation in nature is a seemingly invisible microscopic progress, so powerful that taken together it maintains the whole Earth daily.

When we are receptive to this natural exchange, we become part of the creative power that is bigger than us. This is the effortless guidance we have available to us if we align with our own energy and allow natural forces to amplify it. The giving and receiving is never-ending if we allow it to be. Our body knows this flow naturally, but behind the window we're more or less disconnected from it.

Immerse yourself in nature and align with the natural creation of it all, instead of pushing to make solutions to show up in the way you want them to.

You may argue that your inner voice and what you hear is sometimes harsh, judgmental, and never satisfied. That's your inner *critic* speaking, which is a never-ending stream of chatter based on past experiences, conditioning, assumptions, and interpretations. As we discussed in a previous chapter, the inner critic is hired by the mind and ultimately the ego.

The inner voice often gets overridden by the inner critic because we believe that the inner critic, or our thoughts, is the only voice there is. Thoughts run by the ego can contribute to changing viewpoints, feelings of doubt, and inconsistent negative self-talk that is focusing on the external.

In research conducted by HeartMath, "A common report from people who practice being more self-aware of their inner signals is that the heart communicates a steady stream of intuitive information to the mind and brain. In many cases, we only perceive a small percentage of intuitive information or choose to override the signals because they do not match our more egocentric desires."[17]

---

[17] "Science of the Heart: Exploring the Role of the Heart in Human Performance: An Overview of Research Conducted by the HeartMath Institute," HeartMath Institute, Chapter 11, Last accessed Nov 2, 2021, https://www.heartmath.org/research/science-of-the-heart/intuition-research/.

Your inner voice is that still, small voice within that is there to help guide and direct your life always in a *positive* direction.

Another name for your inner voice is your "gut feeling," a bodily sense that can be hard to put into words but exists to help you navigate your way through any tough decision.

Your intuition is your immediate sense of something as it comes through an intuitive hit. That's no need to think it over or get another opinion—you just know. Your intuition is your inner knowing and is characterized by abundance, confidence, and fulfillment. When you are trusting your intuition, you are trusting yourself.

A definition of intuition developed by HearthMath suggests that there are three types of intuition. The first type is implicit learning, which is basically things we have learned in the past that we forgot. The second type is energetic sensitivity, which is basically how we respond to energy, for example, sensing someone's aura standing behind us without us seeing the person. The third type is non-local intuition, which could be defined as downloads related to the inherent interconnectedness of everything in the universe.[18]

Everyone can learn how to listen to and increase their trust in their intuition, and there are many ways to do so. One of the techniques I teach my clients who want to increase their trust in their intuition is intuitive journaling. Following meditation, when the mind is not active, it's easy to stay in that subconscious space while letting the messages come through.

The trick is to not to pay attention to the meaning of what comes down on the paper or what topic arises; rather, wait and just observe the words coming down on the page, or out through your mouth if you prefer to speak out loud and record it. Everyone is different. Trust that your preference for writing or speaking is just right for you.

The practice of intuitive journaling can be frustrating for some because our minds are so used to interfering and having a say in whether what's said or written is right or wrong and so on. Therefore, practicing meditation is highly recommended so that you can learn to soften the urge to get the mind involved.

We are highly conditioned to deal with distractions and do more than one thing at a time, which does not help us connect with the inner voice. The inner voice itself is a direct connection to our soul,

---

[18] *Ibid.*

and within that space, there's no distraction. It just is one stream of consciousness where distraction is a non-issue. The connection with our inner voice can be a very liberating experience, and it leaves a sensation of expansion.

Another opportunity as you expand your intuition even more, is to commune with your guides in spirit. Your guides are always with you and want to communicate with you. There are many ways you can receive messages from your guides. One great way is to use divination tools such as oracle and tarot cards, and in my experience meditation and intuitive journaling is a powerful way to receive messages. According to an article in MindBodyGreen, for most people, the invitation is to start recognizing the communication that's already happening.[19]

When we are receptive to this natural exchange, we become part of the creative power that is bigger than us. This is the effortless guidance we have available to us if we align with our own energy and allow natural forces to amplify it. The giving and receiving is never ending if we allow it to be. Our soul knows this flow of interaction naturally.

In the space in communion with our inner voice, we have a voice. A bold voice. And we can't hide anymore from the vulnerable side of us that often gets put away while trying to be externally successful. That bold voice of ours is our truth. And we know it when we hear it. It's the voice of our heart and our inner knowing. That's when we start to trust.

And when we start to trust our intuition, there may be some profound insights, such as:

"Yes, I DO love walking in the woods to take in the energy."

"Yes, I DO love deep conversations more than anything."

"Yes, I CAN talk at length about how important self-awareness is."

And "I can FEEL the direction I'm going in now."

---

[19] Tanya Carroll Richardsson, "6 Types Of Spirit Guides & How To Communicate With Them," Mbgmindfulness, Last accessed Nov 2, 2021, https://www.mindbodygreen.com/0-17129/how-to-effectively-communicate-with-your-spirit-guides.html.

Exercise:
Intuitive Journaling

Intuitive journaling is journaling on steroids with a pinch of inner virtual reality! This exercise could also be done by recording your voice instead of writing.

Bring out your favorite journal and pen. Find a comfortable place where you can sit undisturbed for at least 20 minutes.

Close your eyes and allow yourself to sense your body. Imagine you are connecting with the Earth.

As you meditate for few minutes, focus on listening to any subtle sounds around you and let your mind follow those sounds.

Open your eyes halfway, pick up your pen, and start writing without thinking about what to write.

Just write down what comes up.

Do not read what you write; just watch the words come to the page.

Continue to write without interruption as long as you wish.

If you feel nothing is coming through, close your eyes and return to listening.

When you feel ready, put down your pen.

Read what you wrote.

What stands out to you?

Does anything surprise you?

What can you learn from what came through?

9

Nature and Abundance

It's so incredibly HARD!! This was the second day of my experiment. I sat completely still with my feet connected to the Earth. The Sun shined its energy through me and down into the ground. I was just sitting still.

The wind was blowing a gentle breeze. The branches of the trees slowly moved in random directions. The wind's movement was like the bubbling joy I felt inside when I was a child playing outside and skipping around.

I wasn't holding my phone, eating, or drinking—just observing myself and my environment for fifteen minutes uninterrupted.

My mind wanted to focus on what I was going to do later. Each time my mind drifted away, I brought myself back to noticing a leaf moving in the wind or a bird flying across the sky. With the air moving around me, my feet took on the pulse of the Earth.

My breath started to become slower and slower. I sat calmly on my chair with my hands in my lap. The wind continued to play around with the trees and with my inner world. I intentionally tried to keep my attention on one leaf for a little while longer.

Next, a thought came through. *Isn't the fifteen minutes up yet??* That was shortly followed by: *Please tell me it can't be that much longer.*

My attention on the trees and the wind moving the branches and leaves was interrupted.

I checked my phone. Immediately, my mind said, *Why did I do that?* and I judged myself. The restlessness rose within me. I quickly put down the phone on the ground again.

OK, back to being present.

I took a deep breath, and my eyes searched for the perfect leaf. The leaves continued to play with the wind, or vice versa. A gust of wind blew directly in my face, dividing my hair and exposing my forehead. It felt good.

I took another deep breath through my nose. I couldn't smell anything, whatsoever, so I inhaled again, now deeper, with the intent of at least smelling *something*.

Maybe I can trace a little dirt smell or grass smell, maybe!? I wasn't sure. This took me by surprise. *No sense of smell?!*

Nothing!

It dawned on me that I might have been walking through life, not using my sense of smell that often. I knew I could recall the smell of coffee in the morning, but that was about it. I took another deep breath through my nose.

This time, I took the time to inhale deeply and intentionally to take in the smell of what was around me. Now I noticed the familiar smell of cut grass. I thought to myself: *This is how life is experienced. I love the smell of cut grass!*

As I continued to sit on my cushioned chair outside, I felt immense gratitude and pride in myself for actually doing this experiment.

Fifteen minutes of presence.

My sense of smell is back. Phew!

I don't know why I had to check the time on my phone when I knew I had an alarm set, but I only checked the time on my phone once in fifteen minutes. That's an accomplishment, for sure!

All while nature just continued in flow.

Back to Nature

What is your relationship with nature?

There is nothing more abundant than our Earth and the natural energy flow that we have access to when we're in nature. When we intentionally notice the richness that is naturally around us, we're shown the energy of abundance and an experience that deepens and enriches the present moment. The stability, inner peace and reassurance that nature offers us is important when we're in the midst of rapid evolution and change.

Professor Peter H. Kahn at the University of Washington says, "We need to deepen the forms of interaction with nature and make it more immersive."[20] What he alludes to here is that there are indications that modern living doesn't encourage us to physically interact with nature to the same extent as previous generations.

Studies have shown that spending time in nature can have a positive effect on blood pressure, reduce stress hormone levels, reduce nervous system arousal, enhance immune system function, increase self-esteem, reduce anxiety, and improve mood.[21] Spending the majority of our time indoors, on the other hand, has potential impacts on our health, such as fatigue, insomnia, anxiety, and depression.[22]

By spending time in nature, we can invite ourselves to align with the vastness and unlimited creativity of the Earth and become one with it and a feeling that there's nothing missing; it's already perfection. In nature we open and align our own heart energy with the energy of nature, which can extend our sensation of ease and flow even beyond the time spent in nature.

Abundance is right in front of us if we want to tap into it. And in nature we can experience abundance in its true form, existing in real time. The abundance found in nature is the same quality of energy that we're looking for when we want abundance in other areas of life, whether it's the energy of money or inner happiness.

Often, we refer to perceived roadblocks to access abundance, but the question becomes, why don't we believe that abundance is already around us every day?

---

[20] University of Washington, "Regularly Immersing Yourself in Nature Can Help Health and Wellbeing," WUrban@UW, Last accessed Nov 2, 2021, https://depts.washington.edu/urbanuw/news/regularly-immersing-yourself-in-nature-can-help-health-and-wellbeing/.

[21] Jim Robbins, "How Immersing Yourself in Nature Benefits Your Health," Yale Environment 360, Last accessed Nov 2, 2021, https://e360.yale.edu/features/ecopsychology-how-immersion-in-nature-benefits-your-health.

[22] Lauren Cahn, "You're Spending Too Much Time Inside if This Happens to Your Body," Health Digest, Last accessed Nov 2, 2021. https://www.healthdigest.com/281265/youre-spending-too-much-time-inside-if-this-happens-to-your-body/.

Perhaps it's because we can see the beauty of nature in the form of a beautiful flower or a majestic mountain with our own eyes. It may be because it's harder to believe and trust when we can't physically see the beauty of our true self and the Universe. Essentially, the energy is the same within us as in nature.

When we're present in nature, we heighten our intuition naturally so that we can return to trusting what we sense and feel in concert with everything living around us. For thousands of years, our primitive ancestors survived (and even thrived) in harsh living conditions because they constantly pushed the limits of their ability to perceive the world and make decisions. These decisions relied on heightened senses and intuition to avoid being hunted, to find food and shelter. This deep knowledge and seamless living with nature provided solutions for survival and healing, which is rooted in using all the five senses to their fullest capacity. For example, smelling and tasting nature's plants to determine what is edible and what is not. Observing birds and other animals and their language to understand natural laws. Or being in the presence of trees for wisdom and calm.[23]

Understandably, the way we interact with the outdoors and nature has been impacted in many ways in favor of modern values and pursuit of success. Fortunately, in our modern Western lives, the majority of us do not have to rely on nature or use our five senses for survival; instead we are now seeking other ways to feel more alive and present as we strive to expand our experience of life.

Several studies indicate that being outside in nature for just 20 minutes a day is enough to significantly boost vitality levels. But interestingly, being outdoors, such as being outside in absence of nature, was not the same as being immersed in and interacting with nature, for example, hiking in the woods.[24]

So how can you embrace nature to help you heighten your intuition, nourish your energy, and increase your well-being? The opportunity to be intentional with your interaction with nature and its

---

[23] Brian Mertins, "Beginner's Guide to Developing Intuition With Rewilding," Nature Mentoring, Last accessed Nov 2, 2021, https://nature-mentor.com/intuition-and-rewilding/.

[24] University of Rochester, "Spending time in nature makes people feel more alive, study shows," ScienceDaily, Last accessed November 1, 2021, https://www.sciencedaily.com/releases/2010/06/100603172219.htm.

inhabitants doesn't have to mean a weeklong hike; it can be taking a break from work and going outside for five minutes, or purchasing a crystal holding a certain vibration that is beneficial for you and placing it on your desk or by your nightstand. Crystals are a wonderful way to tune into nature intentionally at home. They also serve specific healing purposes and can cleanse the energy of your environment. The important part here is to incorporate the perspective of nature in your daily experience in some way.

Another aspect of nature is the natural cycles that are constantly moving through their stages. The seasons, of course, come to mind. The moon cycle (and other celestial bodies too) also impacts nature, for example, in the form of tidal water. If the entire ocean is affected by this cycle, don't you think that you're being affected too? Being aware of and tuning into the moon cycle can enhance your awareness and connection to nature and the Earth as well as guide you to be aware of energy shifts occurring throughout the year.

Heart-centered living is calling us back out in nature. By intentionally connecting with nature, we also activate our heart energy and intuition naturally. When we return indoors after a nature walk or time spent hugging trees, we bring a greater sense of calm and balance into our homes.

It's a win-win!

Exercise:
Tune into Nature's Abundance

This exercise is a practice in staying present and deepening your connection with nature and the natural abundance that exists in nature.

Find a comfortable place to sit, preferably outside.

Sit directly on the ground if possible. If you are inside, sit by a window.

Set a timer for 10 minutes.

Visualize yourself connecting with the Earth for a few minutes.

Open your eyes and begin to notice what is around you.

Maybe you see a tree. Maybe you see a butterfly flying by. Maybe there's grass or water where you sit, or a rock that looks interesting.

Select one focus point, for example, a tree.

Notice the details of the leaves on the tree.

Notice how the leaves move in the wind.

Keep noticing the details and keep the focus on the experience.

When you feel you want to shift your focus to another element of nature, feel free to do so.

Follow what inspires you, and don't stop noticing until the 10 minutes are up.

10
The Body's Wisdom

> *"If you're not aware of what your body needs,*
> *you can't take care of it."*
> — Bessel van der Kolk

It was still dark outside one morning in February. My body felt a bit stiff as I slowly sat down on my yoga mat in my bedroom. The diffuser I had just filled up was buzzing quietly as the vapor shot up in the air. I stretched my arms up and moved from side to side to release some of the tension in my spine.

I reached over for a small bottle of sesame oil, which I had heated up, and some citrus and peppermint essential oils, which helped me wake up and reminded me of summer. I felt curious. *I wonder what messages I'll receive from my body today...*

I thought to myself, *This is one of the best times of the day.* I cupped my hand and poured a quarter-size pool of sesame oil into my hand. The golden oil felt smooth and warm against my skin. With one hand I unscrewed the top of the citrus essential oil and put a couple of drops into the pool of sesame oil. After the citrus, I added two drops of peppermint. I put my palms together and then directly onto my feet.

I slowly started to massage my left foot with both hands, going deep into the sole of my foot, finding any sensitive spots. The slow circles around my ankles reminded me to be gentle. With my attention on my left foot for a few minutes, I asked my body a few questions: "What is your message for me today?" "What do you need more of?" "What do you need less of?"

I listened to the answers. They were profoundly wise.

Forgotten Wisdom

For the longest time, I didn't view my body as wise. I saw my body as a working machine that shouldn't have a problem carrying heavy grocery bags, frenetically vacuuming a house in less than half an hour, or running up and downstairs a thousand times for something that was forgotten.

In my opinion, my body's job was to be there, ready to go when I wanted to do something. My body was supposed to be strong and tolerate anything from a day full of stress, to a sometimes-two-hour commute, to skipping a meal. It could just keep going, like me.

My body was not there to be asked any questions or to have an opinion, and it definitely wasn't there to teach me something.

Now, my body is a wise teacher that houses my legacy and wisdom, not just in this life but in the DNA from past generations too.

How can you tap into your body's wisdom?

Recently, my daughter hurt her thumb in a volleyball match. It looked bad, and she had ice on it when she came home. The first thing I asked her was: "Do you think it's broken?"

Without hesitation she said, "No, Mom, it's not broken." Her body knew it was not broken, and she trusted that.

In today's society we are encouraged to consult a doctor as soon as we believe we have a reason to, instead of first asking the body what the issue is. We defer the answer to a textbook rather than listen to the natural repository of wisdom that is housed inside of us.

Part of knowing ourselves deeply and fully in a heart-centered way is to embody our true selves, and to do this, we need to know the ins and outs of our bodies. I'm not talking about just knowing our bodies' medical histories but actually knowing what our bodies need without having someone else telling us.

Heart-centered living requires connecting with the wisdom of our bodies complemented by modern medical practice and ancient alternative healing modalities for a better holistic health outcome.

As suggested by Shen and Walker in 2019, "The mind thinks. The body feels—and therefore can offer a unique and valuable wisdom. Just as seeing and hearing are two distinct senses which supply us with valuable information, so too, the body gives us different feedback than the mind."[25]

This inner knowing of our bodies' signals is part of living from a place of intuition. We often hear people say, "My gut feeling is..." That's exactly what it is. Our intuition and body wisdom are closely linked. The body signals to us that there's something we need to know and pay attention to.

When our mind is in the driver's seat, we often automatically seek answers from external sources without tapping into the message of the body. We often allow ourselves to override the body's signals in favor of an answer or reason that the mind already has made up a conclusion about. When we are disconnected from our body's wisdom, we sometimes rely on our ego, in belief that we're superior to our inner knowing and body wisdom.

Have you ever disregarded your body's signals, favoring the mind's promises of quick solutions? What were the consequences?

How do we get closer to trusting this inner knowing of what the body needs, not just occasionally, in certain situations when it comes to our health matters, but ALL the time, in a variety of situations, from nutrition to healing?

Our intuitive are abilities associated with our body's wisdom and primarily the third eye energy center, located between the eyebrows, are connected to the heart energy. Because the third eye is located in the head, we automatically assume that this is a domain of the mind, when, in fact, it is a center of intuition.

There is no better feeling than the one of just knowing, and the body is the vehicle for this sensation to happen. An article by *Wanderlust* describes this state perfectly: "By paying attention to the physical responses your body has, not just the emotional ones, you become aware of how your body is like a life coach that is constantly working to guide you to a state of wellbeing."[26]

---

[25] Leonard Shen, et al., "Body Wisdom and Mindfulness Tools to Enhance Workplace Performance," ABA 13th Annual Labor and Employment Conference, November 9, 2019, https://www.americanbar.org/content/dam/aba/events/labor_law/2019/annual-conference/papers/body-wisdom-and-mindfulness.pdf.

[26] Kara Fujita Jovic, "Tapping Into the Mind–Body Connection," Wanderlust, Last accessed Nov 2, 2021, https://wanderlust.com/journal/tapping-the-bodys-inherent-wisdom/.

Connecting with our body's wisdom starts with inviting our disconnected body back to communicate with us. This involves slowing down to invite back all the bodily senses to give us information that is beyond reason or mental hypothesis.

Understandably, getting back in touch with our body can feel difficult sometimes, not only because we have forgotten how to but also because we might feel resistance towards what kinds of body memories we'll come across. An important aspect of this is to explore our body wisdom with compassion, as sometimes the body can store difficult emotional memories. This can show up as an instant release of emotions and energy in the body. When the body is releasing a difficult memory in the form of pent-up energy, it may show up as a sudden emotion. For example, I have had students in yoga class share with me that they suddenly felt overwhelmed by deep sorrow during a yoga sequence involving a certain body part and experiencing a physical energy release that resulted in a lighter sensation in the entire body afterward.

For years, I separated my body from my mind. Ninety-nine percent of the time, my mind was running the show until I was both mentally and physically exhausted. Not anymore.

Just by asking yourself what your body needs, you'll create space to allow your body to speak to you. Maybe the lower back is tensed up? Maybe you're having a headache? Or maybe your stomach hurts? That's all body-talk.

Listen to it!

In addition, when you pay attention to your body and how it feels when you're around other people, you allow yourself to learn what your body signals to you about that person without engaging the mind.

From there you also have the opportunity to protect your energy from being given away to another person. Keeping your energy during the day is the key to warding off exhaustion.

If you want to connect back to and experience your body, I recommend any practice that has to do with *intentional* movements, such as gentle yoga, intuitive dance, breathwork, or spontaneous laughing. Even leaning against a tree, asking it to share its wisdom with you, is a form of intentional movement. Be creative!

The intention behind engaging and awakening the body's senses fully is to become more aware of the signals the body is sending and allow the mind to take a step back.

According to Harvard Health Publishing, a regular yoga practice can bring insights about our body that carries over beyond the actual practice, such as enhanced awareness related to food, and can enhance satisfaction with the overall body.[27]

When our body's response is clear, it is our truth. Within that energy of inner knowing and trust, there isn't any back and forth or anxiety; there is only clarity, calm, and compassion. By including the body's perspective of life into our experience through its sensations, we will be able to connect even deeper to our true selves.

---

[27] Harvard Medical School, "Yoga Benefits Beyond the Mat," Harvard Health Publishing, https://www.health.harvard.edu/staying-healthy/yoga-benefits-be-yond-the-mat.

Exercise:
Body Scan

In this exercise, you'll use your intuition to communicate with the body to receive messages.

Find a spot where you won't get disturbed.

You may want to lay down or sit comfortably.

Take a few deep breaths in through your nose, bringing your attention to the inflow and outflow of the air.

Ask your body to let you know which part needs attention right now.

Place one hand there.

Ask your body again. It may indicate a second area of your body that needs attention.

Place your other hand there.

Imagine that your hands are transmitting healing energy to the places on your body that needs healing or release.

When you feel ready to move your hands to different spots, ask for direction from your body and let your hands find new spots.

Continue as long as you wish.

If you repeat this exercise over a number of days, you may find that your body is directing you to come back to certain spots. Take note of the message that the body is giving you and notice if there are repeating messages.

If the messages are repeating themselves, consider this a sign that it may be something important that you need to explore further.

11
Signs and Synchronicity

"In every moment, the Universe is whispering to you. You're constantly surrounded by signs, coincidences, and synchronicities, all aimed at propelling you in the direction of your destiny."
— Denise Linn

In my early adulthood, I wasn't giving a huge amount of effort and thought to what I was going to become. I had a few ideas of what I wanted, but more ideas about what I didn't want.

As I was looking for an internship towards the end of finishing up my degree in chemical engineering, I had put out some thoughts out to professors at school, my parents, and others of what I was looking for but nothing specific.

One day, the idea came up from a friend of my cousin that I could potentially ask someone that he knew who worked at a pharmaceutical company. He suggested I ask if they were taking interns at any of their research and development departments.

The next morning, with an innocent heart, I picked up the phone to call the human resources contact I was given. To my surprise, after being transferred to the hiring researcher, who later became my boss, and speaking to him briefly, my request for an internship was accepted on the spot. He said, "Sounds good. When can you start?"

Wow! No applications, no visits, it just came together and happened as if it was meant to be. But I didn't think much more about how it all came together then. It was the start of my corporate experience, and I was led into a career that shaped my adulthood for many years.

I think many of us have the sensation of being guided in life from time to time, but we often don't realize it until afterward.

In hindsight, with that internship coming into my life with very little effort on my part, I can clearly see that I was gently guided by the Universe along my life path.

Fast forward to a few years ago. I knew that something different was happening to me when I started to notice synchronicity in real time, not just in hindsight.

In the past, I could think of things that had happened and realize: "Oh, yes! That happened then because of this and that...." But when I started to notice synchronicities in real time, however, I knew I was guided in the direction of my life's true purpose.

One night, I was surfing around on a website and came across a webpage with an invitation to quite an expensive three-day spiritual transformation workshop in New York City.

All of a sudden, a feeling of "I have to DO this!" came over me. Up until then, it had been quite out of character by me to just sign up for things off the cuff, let alone not knowing if I could take the day off on Friday that attendance required. The idea of going by myself to New York City felt exciting and adventurous, and sure enough, I signed up.

This workshop was like nothing I had been drawn to before in my entire life. I had been to many industry conferences in my career, so travelling by myself and experiencing new things anywhere in the world was not new to me, but what was new was the vibe. The vibe at this workshop was different. The people were different. There was a genuine interest among the participants in how we could help each other to grow, expand, and ultimately serve others on their life paths.

Imagine three full days of expansion of self-awareness, learning about spirituality and learning from others, having deep conversations with like-minded people who were also are in the process of asking themselves deep questions.

Most importantly, the vibe of the people that attended the workshop was something I had never experienced before. I made lifelong friends there. I drove home from New York City elated. I played music so loud in the car, feeling a newfound freedom I hadn't let out in many, many years. I even saw a billboard on the way home, another synchronistic event, which was literally screaming at me, saying, "Don't wait. Make a plan!"

When I came home from this weekend in New York City, my husband asked me, "What did you guys do at this workshop? You're glowing!"

This workshop was the seed of purpose I had been waiting for.

Guided on Your Soul Path

How can you notice signs and synchronicities in your life? An article published by Well+Good suggests that the tricky part is simply learning how to spot the signs and synchronicities and interpret their messages, and it suggests learning about the spiritual meanings of the synchronicities to understand what they're trying to tell you.[28]

Signs are common—whether it's noticing number combinations or the repeated appearance of certain birds or animals. Often there are spiritual meanings to specific signs, and the synchronicity of when and where they are noticed also plays a role. One of the best use of signs and synchronicities is to help support you trust what you already are being told by your intuition.

In psychology, synchronicity is defined as the occurrence of meaningful coincidences that seem to have no cause.[29] Synchronicity can be further explained as the act of noticing certain meaningful things, which are there anyway, but which we otherwise would not notice. In my opinion, synchronicities are available to us at all times, as we are part of the universal flow of energy, but we may or may not notice the synchronicities. But when we do, they nudge us forward in the direction of our soul path.

Sometimes that experience is grueling, sometimes that experience is elated, but it's always perfect.

I don't like the word "perfect" because it brings me back to that anxious feeling of pushing ahead like a sharp arrow through the dark, when it's really time to stop, but in the context of our soul path, the word "perfect" feels like light, like soft cotton, a white cloud that is holding us by the hand and guiding us forward.

---

[28] Jessica Estrada, "No, It's Not Just a Coincidence—Here's How To Spot and Decode Spiritual Synchronicities," Well+Good, Last accessed Nov 2, 2021, https://www.wellandgood.com/what-does-synchronicity-mean-spiritually/.

[29] Jane Piirto, "Synchronicity and Creativity," *Encyclopedia of Creativity* (Second Edition), (Cambridge: Academic Press, 2011), 409-413.

Answering the Call

Our awakening to our true self through our heart and intuition doesn't have to be noticeable to anyone else, at first.

It could be as simple as starting to notice signs that are given to us or synchronicities that confirm an inner feeling that we've been carrying for a while to allow us to trust the inner message even more.

It could be through an inkling in our body that tells us to go a certain direction or that we need to have something double-checked instead of following what everyone else is suggesting.

It could be the connection with the energy of nature around us that helps us to gain clarity in the moment rather than trying to figure it out by asking for advice.

It could be that intuitive hit that brings us the brilliant solution we're looking for to a problem or an instant spark of inspiration and inner knowing that it's going to be fine, instead of planning six months ahead and double checking everything.

It could be the awareness of someone's intention through the energy that they emit, rather than listening to their words.

When the Universe is calling you to reveal your next step on your soul path, answer it. When you start to notice changes in your preferences, whether it's music, food, or even how long you stay up at night, align with it.

The idea is to allow ourselves to step into a safe bubble with the inquiry: "How could I serve myself and others around me better?" and genuinely be curious about it. That's when we learn about the transformation to come.

When we align to our own natural energy, our inner voice can come forward, and we can live from our heart's energy. It feels like reinvention, but it's funny to call it that when we are already perfectly aligned with the Universe.

Our life purpose is always present from the moment we open our eyes in this world. The hardships we need to go through are narrow passages that truly shape us and mold us into our next phase. It's hard sometimes to believe that our life's journey is perfect, but it is.

Exercise:
Noticing Signs and Synchronicities

The Universe is giving you signs all the time. The question is whether you notice them or not and learn how to interpret them.

Start small. The trick is to be observant and decide that you're open to noticing any sign that is given to you over a specific time.

Start with 15 minutes, or pick a day.

Say to yourself, "I'm open to any signs today that are supportive and for the highest good for all."

You can also ask for a certain object or image to be shown to you specifically. A feather, an animal, an insect, or a number are common signs that our guides are using to communicate with us.

Practice noticing and don't have any expectations about time or how. Patience is a virtue when it comes to signs and synchronicities.

Once you have received a few signs, you'll just move on to notice the signs as they come in.

Especially in the beginning, you may also want to record these signs in your journal.

PART 3:
Multidimensional Living:
The Seven Shifts

"Only from the heart you can touch the sky."
— Rumi

A more fulfilling life starts with ourselves, no matter our past or current situation. There is endless possibility to transform our lives and expand beyond what we believe we can do and experience. There is an opportunity to elevate our current reality to a higher perspective sourced from our true self and the connection with the Universe, our heart energy, our intuition, and our body wisdom.

On a practical level, this is a shift in perspective away from stress, multitasking, and feeling like we are disconnected from ourselves as a result of conforming to the expectations of our mind-driven ego and social norms.

To shift into living from the heart and intuition is to live in the present moment, as opposed to the past or the future. It is with our senses we activate our ability to be part of something beyond the physical experience, but it's with trust we believe that our own power can bring us to our truth.

Our soul's truth is the same as the essence of the Earth and the Universe. In Part 3, you"ll traverse through a series of seven shifts, highlighting how you can expand beyond what you know and live a multidimensional life.

Shift 1: From the Comfort Zone to Commitment

Change can be terrifying, but often only before we decide to begin. At a crossroads we face the choice, and we ask ourselves if it's time for a change that will last. In Chapter 12, you are encouraged and offered to get out of the comfort zone and declare your commitment to making a leap to change into a more fulfilling life.

Shift 2: From Disconnected to Self-Aware

When we turn our focus from the external world to the internal world, something magical happens! The discovery of our inner conversation and our natural energy expression is a life-changing insight for many. In Chapter 13, you'll discover something new about yourself and what's really going on within. Then, decide if you like it or not.

Shift 3: From Codependency to Sovereignty

Untangle the web of the past that holds you back from your uniqueness so that you can get know who you truly are. When you return to acknowledge your inner child's needs, you become energetically sovereign. In Chapter 14, you are shown one way to stand in your power.

Shift 4: From Learning to Embodying

You know you are transforming when you are experiencing what you envisioned. Embodying involves getting out of the tendency to take in more information and move deeper into the action of becoming. In Chapter 15, your inner transparency is developed so that you go from learning to embodying your truth, instead of continuing to live the life you *thought* you wanted.

Shift 5: From Logic to Wisdom

In the richness of wisdom is where your true self arrives. Logic keeps us moving forward but with no end. In Chapter 16, you are encouraged to make the shift from logic to wisdom by connecting with the joy in your heart.

Shift 6: From Pushing to Manifesting

It is possible to make an instant shift to manifesting what you want! The belief that we need to struggle to receive is keeping us from truly expanding effortlessly. In Chapter 17, you are invited to make a shift from pushing to manifesting in an instant and start to receive in a new way.

Shift 7: From Individual to Multidimensional

When you relate to dimensions beyond the physical, it is a big leap towards oneness, harmony, and balance to stay in union with both the Earth and the Universe. A distracted and stressed way of living cannot constantly hold this energy. In Chapter 18, you are invited to explore your multidimensional self, creating a daily spiritual practice to help you consistently integrate your experience.

12

Shift 1: From the Comfort Zone to Commitment

> *"Commitment is an act, not a word."*
> — Jean-Paul Sartre

A number of years ago, like many evenings before, I caught myself standing in the kitchen, scrolling on my phone for an email from work. I felt exhausted. I'd lost my own energetic flow, as I'd spent all this time reading emails in the last hour by only moving my thumb! I wouldn't have had any idea of much time I'd spent scrolling back and forth unless the screen-time alert had gone off. *Ugh! Such a waste of energy. This has to stop*, I thought.

I thought I did the right thing by working harder to become someone, and that an improved life would emerge as a result. But all it did was to pull me away from my natural energy flow.

As I dragged myself back into my office, it was late in the evening, I knew I had to take a hard look at why I was spending time working late at night after the kids were in bed. Night after night, I kept going and going. I didn't acknowledge that I needed more balance in my life. What I truly needed was time away from work to regain my sense of self and get out of the exhaustion.

I felt resistance towards what I was doing, and it meant that I wasn't in alignment with my energy.

My body said, "NOT another night, PLEASE!"

My ego said, "Don't complain. Just get on with it."

And so I did for yet another night. I was getting more and more frustrated each night of the week because there was no balance between energy expenditure and replenishing my energy or maintaining it.

Fortunately, I discovered my body to be the wisest of wise because long before I allowed myself to acknowledge my reality and step away from the computer, my body said, "No more!" My body had been clearly signaling the imbalance and need for a change for some time, but my very strong ego, fueled by a demanding work role, kept me going back night after night.

A few months later, as I sat there at my desk, I was witnessing my rock bottom. I felt like I had a blindfold over my eyes. It felt like I was looking up to the sky but not seeing it. There was nothing to look at and aim for anymore. The career I had poured my energy into all these years was gone. It wasn't that I couldn't get another job; my self-identity had been ripped away. I knew somewhere deep down that the commitment to my career was gone *within* me. And with that feeling of loss of self-identity, my commitment to staying in the comfort zone was gone too.

The Comfort Zone

What does it mean to get out of the comfort zone? We hear about getting out of our comfort zones all the time, and it's a nice concept, but what does it really mean?

The phrase "comfort zone" was coined by management thinker Judith Bardwick in her 1991 book *Danger in the Comfort Zone*. By her definition, "The comfort zone is a behavioral state within which a person operates in an anxiety-neutral condition, using a limited set of behaviors to deliver a steady level of performance, usually without a sense of risk."[30] And, as outlined by an article in *Positive Psychology*, the comfort zone is where we feel safe and in control and an element of fear and learning is part of the path to soul growth.[31]

[30] Judith M. Bardwick, *Danger in the Comfort Zone: From Boardroom to Mailroom: How to Break the Entitlement Habit That's Killing American Business,* (New York: American Management Association, 1995).

[31] Oliver Page, "How to Leave Your Comfort Zone and Enter Your 'Growth Zone'," Positive Psychology, Last accessed Nov 2, 2021, https://positivepsychology.com/comfort-zone/.

My entire childhood was built upon staying in the comfort zone.

Everyone was pretty much living a similar life as time went by; at least, that's how it appeared to me growing up. Taking risks and moving out of the safety bubble of a small town were rare occasions. Once someone got a job, they usually stayed in that job forever unless the company shut down. So, based on that template, the thought of shifting into something completely different was very farfetched for me. By early adulthood, very few people I knew had seemingly made a complete turnaround in life to emerge into doing something different.

Personally, after a few broken relationships, a number of mind-driven jobs, and some shallow friendships, the Universe bluntly served up an opportunity for major soul growth for me.

Initially, after the layoff from my job, I felt completely terrified. I didn't want anything to change. I didn't want to change. It felt too scary to go seek the depths of who I was.

Because I had never gone there before. My job was me. When I hit rock bottom, it required me to get still, close my eyes, and look within.

But as I sat there in the midst of the fact that my job was gone, the choice was mine. Did I want to stay in the comfort zone or make a fierce commitment to change?

The circumstances required me to finally ease the tight hold I had around my daily routine and assumptions of what I was capable of. It required me to open up and rediscover my feelings and my creativity and passion that had been buried within me for a long time, or maybe even never felt before.

The situation required me to do things differently, even if I didn't know how. It required me to completely shift the pace of my life, including what and who I was interacting with on a daily basis. It required me to take a free fall out in the unknown inner world without knowing where I'd land.

As we stand there, cracked open, realizing we need to change something about our lives that are no longer working, what do we do? Do we take guidance from a friend, family member, or an expert? Or do we take guidance from our inner voice and our true self? It's one of the loneliest feelings you can ever experience because deep down our soul knows the choice is ours, and only ours.

Often, when we feel stuck and realize something is not working or we struggle, we've disconnected from parts of ourselves, and we don't even realize that we disconnected from them.

Only limited parts of ourselves have been alive, and we have not fully expressed our soul's truth through our innate passion, talents, and gifts. When we are not in connection with our true selves, we don't live a whole life.

But within the struggle, there is always a hidden call for more—to uncover more of who we are and what we're made of at the depths of our souls. As long as we're relying on guidance from others, our true self won't reveal itself fully.

Maybe you have felt the same at some point. Like the one-way lane has suddenly come to a crossroads.

A Commitment to Become Whole

Now it's time to stop remaining in the comfort zone and make the shift into a commitment of change.

When you are committing to yourself to change your habits and ways of living, you have the opportunity to take action and show yourself that you're willing to become whole.

One of the most powerful ways you can make a commitment is to declare it and make it real and visible for yourself and others. It's with a commitment to your journey that transformation truly starts. Up until the day you are all in, it's only going to be a half-baked job.

What happens when you decide with your entire being to commit to becoming willing to change?

You can awaken aspects of yourself that may have been put away, pushed down, or ignored for a long time because these parts have not been welcomed or encouraged by others. When you become willing to change, you start the process of calling back the parts of you that you've disconnected with despite what someone else says.

Now, in this moment of choice, it's time to call back ALL parts of yourself. Call all parts back into your life in their full glory, just the way they were given to you, not only at birth but a long time before this life.

You deserve to feel whole again to live and serve the world by being authentically yourself. It is your birthright.

The commitment we make to ourselves serves as the safety net to the possible fear and learning we have to go through to grow. Here at the crossroads, we stand completely nude, holding space to make a life-changing decision. A decision that has the power to remove the layers of past modification and fill in the corners that were cut out of ourselves along the way.

This is a moment when we can decide to radiate power and compassion at the same time. This is a moment to feel safe in breaking new ground into the unknown, even if it feels uncomfortable, not yet knowing where our limits lie or where this commitment will take us.

I am eternally grateful that I chose to make the commitment to change; to begin a journey of learning how to listen to my inner voice and awaken the parts of me that were dormant rather than continue to stay within in the comfort zone with the endless search for the right answer given by others.

Ultimately, my rock bottom resulted in me stepping through my fear and learning how to identify and reshape my thought patterns, my career, and my habits and routines. Most importantly, the "point of no return" commitment I made to myself helped me elevate myself to step out of the ego's need for control and connect with my heart and intuition to embody my true self.

That unbreakable commitment to myself gave me a sensation of grounding. It helped me put me on a new path that made it possible for me to find my inner voice and surrender to inner peace.

Now it's your turn.

Exercise:
Declare Your Commitment to Yourself

As you read this, tap into your inner level of commitment. Where are you at right now? Is it a GO, or are you hesitating? Will you take the opportunity to make a commitment to change in the area of life that brought you here to this book? Are you willing to?

One of the most powerful ways to declare your commitment is to write it down. Then, put the contract somewhere you can see it and access it every day, perhaps in a special box or in a private space where you easily can find it. To fully commit also comes with making your commitment public to others in some form.

If possible, share your commitment with someone you trust. Treat it as a contract with a date and a signature.

Below is a template that you can use:

MY COMMITMENT TO MYSELF

I am my deepest desire. Today, I declare this commitment to myself to make the changes I want to make to my life.

I welcome _____ into my life:
[describe your intention(s) in as much detail as you can]

★

★

★

So that I can:
[describe what these changes will make possible for you]

★

★

★

Signature: _____
Date: _____

If you're still wishy-washy about committing you may need more time to find out within yourself what would need to happen for you to make the commitment to yourself.

I recommend journaling how you feel about it for a few days to uncover where you truly stand.

Describe the change you want to see in yourself (not in others) to the best of your current inner knowing. Just write down what comes up. There is no right or wrong. It's between you and your true self. It's a commitment to get you going. Use the questions below to get clarity.

If you can't make that full commitment to yourself right now, don't worry; by the end of this book, you will know if the time is right for you and you can come back to this chapter to make a true commitment to yourself.

Clarifying Questions:

1. Describe the issue you feel stuck on.

This can be difficult, and I want you to write it down because we toss around thoughts in our brain, and they remain immaterial; when we write it down, they become tangible.

Second, I recommend not involving others in the answer. Just write about what it is within YOU that you're stuck on.

2. What is the cost to you to stay where you are today?

What is the sacrifice you're making by not moving forward? Is it your happiness? Maybe it's your creativity, motivation, or inspiration that you're sacrificing. What is it that you're not receiving by staying in the comfort zone?

3. What would happen if you made the change?

Often, we resist the unknown. Describe what would happen if you made the change. How would it make you feel? Make sure you describe the impact on you, not how it would impact others.

Respectfully, I totally acknowledge that some decisions involve others, but if you're not clear on what the opportunity means for YOU, you're not going to commit.

I hope you gained a little more clarity and are ready to make a commitment! Now go back to the template and fill it out (or create your own). The important part is that you sign and date it and put it somewhere easily accessible.

13

Shift 2: From Disconnected to Self-Aware

> *"Self-awareness involves deep personal honesty.*
> *It comes from asking and answering hard questions."*
> — Stephen Covey

A s I was cooking dinner and catching up on the latest on social media, I came across someone's beautiful post—a photo of her doing a perfect yoga pose. *"You just need to learn some more, then you can... She looks so perfect. I don't...* Deep sigh... Moving on to the next post.

I turned off the stove, quickly lifting the lid off the pot to see if the rice was cooked. The steam coming out of the pot gave me a quick facelift. *Rice AGAIN...really??!* I felt discouraged. *I need to do something different with our diet. We've been eating the same meals over and over... I should look up some new recipes... Why don't I just wait until next week? Think about it some more...*

I turned around and put the hot pot on the table. "Girls!! DINNER IS READY!" I yelled to make sure they could hear over the TV blaring in the other room. "We have about ten minutes until we need to be in the car for the soccer practice."

My cell phone went off. *Drop everything and answer the call.* I answered the call reluctantly. It was my boss. He was excited, calling to let me know we were in for the bid on the million-dollar contract, the biggest deal in a long time. "Oh GREAT!" I said excitedly as I put the rice in a bowl. As I listened to my boss explaining the additional things that needed to go in the next email back to the customer to win the contract, the girls ate their dinner. My mind was already working on what needed to be done next, and I could feel the anxiety coming over me. *This needs to be done NOW.* I was already thinking about how to craft the email.

Ten minutes had gone by, and the girls were finishing up their dinner. Then, off to soccer with their dad.

The dishes are piling up. Should I leave them for tonight? The dishes always need to be done in the evening… The house needs to be perfect. I cleaned the dishes and later put the girls to bed before hunkering down at my computer to craft that email.

And so it continues…

The Ego Mind's Chatter

The story you just read was an inner conversation where the ego mind is in charge. The background noise of the critical inner chatter constantly at my back.

The ego mind is stubborn. It will shout "I'm GOING to figure it out!!" or the classic "This is how it's ALWAYS been done. It's gotta WORK!" as we scramble during late-night hours. It's that exhausting pattern of the constant chatter of our logical ego mind. The ego is a master at keeping keep us from noticing our inner voice. The mind is focused on problem solving, multitasking, and figuring things out all at the same time. And it goes on and on…

Have you experienced that too? When we are disconnected from our true self, we let the inner conversation drive our lives automatically. We believe the ego mind's stories. We don't question these stories, which are often negative, judgmental, and competitive. And we believe the mind's need to outdo, compete, push, and show the ego's self-importance in light of others' reflections on ourselves and in light of their demands.

Why is increasing our self-awareness important? Well, ask yourself this question: "Do you want to get to know the TRUE you?" If you answer yes to that, then self-awareness is the tool that gives you the opportunity to find out who you are at the soul level. Not the person whom you were told you are. Not the person you thought you were. Not the person you think you have to be. The soul you *really* are.

According to the Center for Spirituality and Healing,[32] "Self-awareness helps you understand what you value and how you perceive the world around you. Once you have perspective on your own values and views, it is easier to accept that others may have differing values and views."

When we get to know our true self, we may realize that we don't agree with the values or the inner chatter we've always had because they make us feel boxed in, or they don't honor our creative side or what we truly enjoy. This is important work, because our values drive everything we take action on.

Similarly, the Center for Spirituality and Healing states: "Becoming self-aware is linked to new possibilities. Once you are self-aware, you can choose new behaviors. With more choices, you develop a broader behavioral palette. This broader palette enables you to act with authenticity and responsiveness even in difficult situations, and to invite others to do the same."[33]

To go from disconnected to gaining self-awareness is an adventure you've never been on before. You start off on a path, walking the trail, and you may think you know the direction. Then, after a while, your feet start to get tired. At first, you might ignore the feeling of being tired and just continue, but as a result you get some huge blisters, and finally, you realize you put the wrong shoes on to begin with.

Some people would choose to keep going until the end without changing anything, and some people would choose to take off the shoes, put a different pair on, and take care of the blisters so that they can heal. These inner wounds may be ones that have been endured for a long time—wearing the wrong shoes but ignoring the problem.

To keep going with the same faulty shoes all the way to the end could be a symptom of being disconnected. Gaining self-awareness is putting on a more comfortable pair of shoes after taking care of the blisters. If you do so, you can continue down your path, hopefully happier and more content. You may even skip down the path!

When we shift into a life where we live from the heart and intuition, we're taking responsibility for everything that happens in

---

[32] "Awareness of Self," Earl E. Bakken Center for Spirituality & Healing, University of Minnesota, Last accessed Nov 2, 2021, https://www.csh.umn.edu/education/focus-areas/whole-systems-healing/leadership/awareness-self.
[33] Ibid.

our life. Taking charge of your life and your decisions may be a hard pill to swallow, but the truth is that if you're taking responsibility for…

* ✳ who you want to be
* ✳ how you want to show up
* ✳ what you want to fill your life with
* ✳ what you want to contribute with

…then you're on your way to getting to the heart of your true self.

So, how do we start making the shift from being disconnected from our true selves to becoming more self-aware?

As discussed in the previous chapter, once we've come to the point of commitment and *truly* are ALL IN, something magical happens. Once we've made the commitment within to step out of the fear and into the unknown, there is a natural urge to learn more about ourselves. By wanting to learn more about our inner world and who we are at the soul level, we have begun the adventure to become self-aware.

I believe that we all come to this life with enormous wisdom but also life lessons that we have decided that we want to work through and experience at the soul level. And we won't tap into past life wisdom, or learn and experience these lessons, unless we become self-aware.

Becoming Aware of Your Family Patterns

The life lessons and the things that we need to become aware of and learn from in this lifetime are already *right in front of us in our daily lives.* I believe that these life lessons are demonstrated to us by the patterns of our close family members. They are playing out what was shown to us during the early years of conditioning.

The dynamic we see in our parents' and relatives' way of handling things is the starting point of our opportunity for our internal learning and to grow in this lifetime.

Our family patterns kind of "just happen," and as young children we are not taught to observe, question, or reflect. We are taught to focus more on external things, such as learning a new math skill in school or playing the piano, having manners, or learning a new language. We don't get education about our inner worlds from an emotional, mental, and spiritual perspective.

Therefore, many of us are not viewing our family dynamics as a source for learning about ourselves. Instead, we often view ourselves as victims of others' behaviors. And unless we become self-aware, we keep repeating the same patterns we witnessed playing out in our parents early on in life. Some things we learned in childhood will be useful later on; other things, not so much.

Here is a great opportunity to ask yourself: "How important is it for me to learn more about myself on an emotional, mental, and spiritual level and become aware of what patterns I keep repeating that are not serving me anymore?"

As long as we stay disconnected, our inner child is maintaining this imprint of those lessons, inherited behaviors, beliefs, or patterns that we are here to change in this life. This cannot happen until we consciously connect back with them in adulthood and begin our journey towards transformation, change, and increased self-awareness.

If you want, revisit Part 1 and the common repeat patterns discussed there. What patterns are you maintaining from your childhood that are not serving you anymore?

Without this awareness, there is no opportunity to change. So look around! The life lessons you need to learn are right in front of you. What are they? The interactions within your immediate family are showing you the behaviors, the beliefs, and the energy exchange that you are here to work on, do differently, evolve away from, adopt, or learn from, all the way from childhood until you leave this life and beyond.

Becoming Aware of Who You Are Energetically

To go deeper in our experience of self-awareness is to learn about who we are *energetically*. This is very different from knowing who we are at the physical level and what family patterns we came from.

As discussed previously, our energy field around us, our aura, is multilayered, extends beyond what is seen, and is connected to the overall well-being of our physical, mental, emotional, and spiritual bodies.

Becoming energetically self-aware requires reconnecting and learning about our natural gifts, our talents. This energetic awareness is not about what we have or what we accomplish; it is about knowing how we run energy through us and how we know to express those talents and gifts. These are not the skills we've learned through training but the talents and gifts we just innately have.

Artist Christina Lonsdale has been photographing people's auras and found that different color combinations may represent different talents expressed through life.[34] Since our natural energy already expresses our uniqueness, why not learn more about it?

If becoming energetically self-aware sounds like a complex science, it's not. Our soul is naturally made up of energy, and the Universe recognizes our energy because we are part of it. If we're disconnected from our natural energy flow, we feel stuck because we are not aligned with the flow of nature or the Universe.

We can learn and become self-aware of our natural energetic expression, including the qualities of our aura. Our aura may be felt by others without us saying a word, and each person has a unique aura. I believe it is helpful to first learn about how we show up energetically when we're stressed. You can simply ask someone how it feels to be around you when you are stressed, and their description of how they feel is your aura in action as you express the energy frequency that stress represents.

As you move into an energy of approaching life from your heart, however, your energy will be felt differently by others, as you may move to express different energetic frequencies as represented by your elevated emotions.

When we were little children, we embodied this natural energy fully, but through life, we participate in society, which is focused on material success. The Universe is just waiting for us to reconnect with our natural energy and align with it instead of working against it. When we work against our own energy, we struggle and feel resistance.

Our experiences and choices in this life unconsciously led us to pull away from our natural energy expression. The good news is that your natural energy expression has never gone away; you've just disconnected from it. In the exercises that follow, you'll reconnect with your natural energy, and you'll get some tips on how to learn more about your energetic imprint from birth.

[34] Fp Julia, "Radiant Human," Bldg25, Last accessed Nov 2, 2021, https://blog.freepeople.com/2016/03/radiant-human/.

Exercise:
A Crash Course in Self-Awareness

Expanding your self-awareness is a lifelong journey, but in this exercise, you'll hopefully learn something new about yourself.

Part I: Test Your Self-Awareness

First, contemplate the below questions:
1. If you had no limits at all, what would be the top three things you would STOP doing today that you know are not serving you anymore?

Then, for each answer, respond to the question below:
2. Why haven't you stopped doing it yet? Take a deep breath and be honest! Notice if the answer you're giving is one of self-awareness or one of blame.

Part II: A Useful Daily Question

If you're in the midst of all the stress, there's this question that can take the edge off any rushed mind. The question is: "What can I learn from this?" It's such a powerful question that will put you right into the present moment.

If you're not asking yourself that question, start today. Without self-awareness, you'll be doing the same thing five years from now. It's through your intention and willingness to learn that you grow, and it's never too late to say YES!

Part III: Going Deeper with Journaling

Journaling is an essential practice for gaining self-awareness. When we journal, our thoughts are coming down on a piece of paper. They become real to us, not just passing thoughts.

In addition, when we journal using our intuition, we become a channel and we bypass our logical mind. Our journal entries can be read again with an objective eye, and we can identify the patterns.

In addition, as we journal, we discover what's *really* going on in our lives. We discover the family patterns that are repeating themselves. For reference, revisit Part 1 for a few common ones as a start.

We may not realize that certain behaviors and opinions are patterns in our lives until we go back and review them—you will see themes emerging. Once we realize what patterns we have, we can do something about them if we want to.

The important part is to notice and reflect on our own patterns and their impact on our lives, positive or negative.

Part IV: Learn About Your Energetic Imprint

There are several different ways to obtain fundamental insights about our own natural unique energy imprints, which we come into this life with. This information is already accessible through ancient and more modern systems that intend to be valuable tools for universal and human understanding. For example, your natal astrology chart is a goldmine of energetic information about you and your unique energy imprint.[35] This ancient system contains the energetic blueprint of our soul's energy in this lifetime based on our unique moment of birth (date and birth time) and location of birth.

In more recent times, newer systems intended to synthesize both ancient and modern sciences have become available to us. One of such systems is Human Design by Ra Uru Hu and another one is the Gene Keys by Richard Rudd.[36,37] Free charts specific to you are available on their respective websites.

Combining these systems gives a deep understanding of our natural energy and progression and is a great starting point to start learning about our natural energy.

So how do we learn about our natural energy imprint?

I highly recommend getting a reading from someone trained and with substantial experience in any or all of these systems to start with. Below are some questions that are great to ask in a reading:

---

[35] Astrodienst, Last accessed Nov 2, 2021, https://astro.com.

[36] Jovian Archive, Last accessed Nov 2, 2021, https://jovianarchive.com/.

[37] The Gene Keys, Last accessed Nov 2, 2021, https://genekeys.com/.

1. What am I naturally talented at?
2. What are the challenges that I may encounter?
3. What is my communication style?
4. What does my energy suggest with regards to relationships?
5. What am I here to learn?
6. How can I best align with my natural energy?

By observing and learning from your family patterns, the readings of your charts, and a dedicated journaling practice, you start to expand your self-awareness, and it becomes a wealth of knowledge of where your unresolved life lessons in this life lie.

14

Shift 3: From Codependent to Sovereign

> *"Don't let the behavior of others destroy your inner peace."*
> —Dalai Lama

I was in my mid-twenties. It was a Sunday night after a long weekend of moving into a new apartment. As I sat with a cup of tea on my new red pull-out couch, I looked around and felt completely me. For the first time ever, I felt the true power of my own unique creativity at play. This past week had been the first time I'd bought a piece of furniture only for myself. More importantly, I had discovered that I could express my unique style and make choices for my new home.

Soaking in all the impressions from the weekend, I felt a new kind of openness within me, mainly due to this newfound feeling of sovereignty.

I didn't have to explain why I had selected the red couch over a black one to anyone; I just picked what I wanted.

I didn't have to negotiate away my opinion and accommodate someone else's. I just had to be me.

Everywhere I looked in my small apartment I could sense the energy of excitement and hope. Bold colors mixed with lightness. My eyes stopped at a photo of my travels to Nepal a few years prior. A wave of emotion welled up within me, and in that moment, I felt the same feeling as I felt hiking in Nepal—I could do anything!! It was an unlimited sensation that I could make the decisions I wanted and create whatever I wanted to create. A bubbling and light feeling of joy and adventure.

I noticed my new music player, and from that point on, it would only play music I wanted to listen to. The thought of it made me smile.

I loved the way my newly decorated bookshelf had come together with items that I had collected over the years that reminded me of things that I valued. Now all of them were gathered as a representation of me.

On one of the shelves I had placed a wooden frame with a quote by Epictetus: *"It's not what happens to you but how you react to it that matters."* That quote completely resonated with me; it represented something important that I just recently had realized—to not see yourself as a victim; rather, see the power and freedom of being in charge of yourself.

In the past, when growing up, I felt that my mom's freely shared opinions about what I should do or wear were suffocating me to the point that I didn't know who I was or what I liked. I felt her opinions were so loudly presented to me that they overshadowed my own essence. I didn't have to think for myself, let alone feel into what was right for me at the time.

But in hindsight, I learned that I had allowed it and for a reason. I had allowed it because one of my life lessons was to become aware that I need to actively work through and learn who I was to release myself from codependency and into sovereignty.

I had to learn how to establish boundaries and speak up for myself. I had to learn not to let others speak for me and to not take someone else's direction on what was right for me.

For the longest time, it was very easy to blame my mother as the reason for the suppression of my own self-love, which was something I felt within myself well into my adult years.

Now, it was as if I wanted to show myself that I, in fact, *could* make decisions for myself and be true to myself, no matter what anyone else said.

Suddenly, I felt the urge to jump up from my couch. My favorite song came on. I turned up the volume and danced by myself to celebrate my newfound inner freedom and return to myself.

I realized that in the past I had listened too much to others' preferences when it came to music, listened to others' opinions about what the best thing to do was, and listened to others' opinions on what to wear or to do next.

This feeling of power coming from within was a very different feeling from before. I felt deep inside me that I was ready for a new chapter of my life, not only materially with new furniture in my apartment but internally too.

Unbounded and free, it felt like I had to make up for the years that I had put myself in the back seat. I bought a new car and went on many adventures.

These were the things I didn't do on my own terms, having been in steady relationships from a young age. But now it was time to find out who I really was from within. For three years, I spent a lot of time with girlfriends, having fun, laughing a lot, shopping, having dinner together, and going out to dance or just hanging out, sunbathing in the summer.

I found my wings, found my inner spark, and found a new sense of excitement and calm within. A new sense of what I was made of that I didn't know before. A key piece to the puzzle on my soul path without someone else's mirror held up in front of me all the time. I found a home in myself for the first time as an adult.

It was a new feeling for me to serve my inner child completely from my own energy, with play, freedom, and sisterhood, without the need to first validate myself through an intimate relationship with another person. I could feel my inner passion and authentic creative force being expressed from within.

The shift from not knowing what my preferences were or what I truly loved to rely on my own heart compass and trust that I have the answers within at all times.

Seeking Answers

How do we come to our answers in life?

Where I grew up in rural Sweden, couples often found each other in or right after high school, got married in their early twenties, and had their first child not long thereafter. As expected, I too had a steady boyfriend since my late teens. I tended to attract relationships where my continued lack of self-identity and low self-esteem could be validated by seeking answers, safety, and identity in another person.

This behavior is not unusual. We tend to seek inner answers to large and small questions in life through external sources of validation.

In today's world, when we don't know the answer to something, we open up our phone or computer and we "Google it" to find an article or book about it. It's great to get information and inspiration from others (including reading this book), but the energy exchange of asking someone else (read Google) is too easy sometimes. We have access to a vast body of knowledge at our fingertips that is external to us, where we can learn more about the experiences *as described by others*.

Another scenario may be that we ask someone we trust what they think about the matter and take their advice or suggestions at face value without inner contemplation.

What may happen is that we may quickly absorb someone else's experience as our own, and then we're on to the next thing because we believe we've solved a problem.

What if someone else's interpretation of the issue isn't what we truly need? Simply, by seeking external validation and stopping at that, we give our power away. The question "Is the solution right for ME?" goes unanswered, despite all that seeking and information gathering.

Codependency

Codependency is a very common life pattern. We can be codependent on a family member, romantic partner, a friend, a colleague, a boss, and so on.

When we're codependent, we may feel lost or doubt ourselves and we may often revisit decisions, constantly asking others for advice. Very Well Health summarizes codependent behaviors nicely: "No interests or values outside the relationship, or having difficulty identifying their own needs, having fear of separation or abandonment and self-worth tied to sacrificing oneself's needs."[38]

One of the fundamental steps on the journey from codependency to sovereignty is finding out what our true values are and what matters to us now. Values are the things that you believe are important in the way you live and work. We may not think about our values every day, but it's essential to get to the bottom of what's behind our own inner

---

[38] Heather Jones, "What Is Codependency?," Verywellhealth, Last accessed Nov 2, 2021, https://www.verywellhealth.com/codependency-5093171.

sense of power. Our values drive everything we do, believe it or not, so this is something we want to be totally clear on. In Brené Brown's book *Dare to Lead* there is a useful list of values, which is downloadable.[39]

Another sign of codependency is that we may feel that other people around us make us stressed; we take in their problems, their problems become ours, and we get upset. While this may be an issue of taking on someone else's energy, a co-dependent person automatically considers someone else's energy above their own. Simply put, the enmeshment of energy in a codependent relationship is evident, which leads to the co-dependent person not standing up for themselves and their own needs.

Codependent individuals may feel that they need to be in control and stay on top of every move in life, including others' lives, in order to be able to succeed.

I used to be so upset when I saw someone do something I knew wasn't right or good for them (such as, from my perspective, eating too much or drinking too much) or I saw them behaving in a way that I felt was only contributing to their problems. Their issue became my focus and worry, and I endlessly tried to get them to see and solve their problems. And beneath it all, I buried my desire to speak my truth and share my opinion of how I felt about the situation.

There was a huge relief within me once I felt I could let go of the need to be one step ahead and be the one pointing out the flaws. It was an amazing feeling of a weight falling off my shoulders—not having to be the one feeling responsible for identifying another person's insights or giving my opinion of what someone else should do or not.

And here's the game-changer…

Through practicing self-awareness, I can now say that I relate to others in a completely different way. I now relate to others through a sense of sovereignty. What I mean by that is that I no longer feel responsible for others' issues. I am no longer someone who takes others' energy, issues, or problems on unless I want to. That is truly a key component of my sense of freedom, independence, and well-being today.

The self-awareness, sensation of sovereignty, and a completely new level of trust in the process of life that I have today is something I wish for everyone.

---

[39] Brené Brown, "Dare to Lead Hub: Workbook, Glossary, and Art Pics," Last accessed Nov 2, 2021, https://daretolead.brenebrown.com/workbook-art-pics-glossary/.

With increased self-awareness, I began to source my answers from within instead of relying on another person's answers or opinions. The answer to our question is within our true self, our consciousness, but if we're disconnected from it and constantly rely on validation, we can't discern whether the answer we receive is right for us.

The soul consciousness of our true self in this lifetime is energy that has been around the block a few times; it's been with us for lifetimes. Our soul consciousness has been with us since the inception of our soul lifetimes back, and what we need to learn in this lifetime has likely been experienced already in some aspect in previous lifetimes. So, instead of relying on external sources for answers to our questions, remember that the answers are within. And if we just listen, we'll realize the answers are full of wisdom.

Getting to Know Your Inner Child

Parts of the answers come from the purest part of ourselves, our inner child. Many of us have an inner child whose needs growing up weren't met in a way that we'd wanted.

One powerful technique that can be used to start to get to know our inner child was described by Lucia Capacchione in her book *Recovery of Your Inner Child*.[40] This technique is based on writing out conversations with our subconscious by using our non-dominant hand as our inner child's voice. A two-way conversation about values and unmet needs can reveal deep insights and healing.

In discussing inner child work, an article published by MindBodyGreen points out that the intention with inner child work is to speak to our inner child through their language, a language that is emotionally based and embodied, rather than expressed through intellectual thoughts and words.[41]

There is a strong link between our connection to creativity and our inner child as well. As a child, you probably did plenty of things just for fun. You didn't have to do them; you just wanted to. But you

[40] Lucia Capacchione, *Recovery of Your Inner Child* (New York: Simon & Schuster, 1991).

[41] Tiffany Trieu, "What Is Inner Child Work? A Guide to Healing Your Inner Child," Mbgmindfulness, Last accessed Nov 2, 2021, https://www.mindbodygreen.com/articles/inner-child-work.

might have a hard time recalling the last time you did something in your adult life simply because it made you happy. Creative activities like coloring, doodling, or painting can help connect you to your inner child. When you let your active mind rest, emotions you usually don't consider can surface.[42]

A conversation with your inner child about what it needs can open up insights about yourself that you hadn't considered before in your adult life.

Becoming Sovereign

Personally, I can't remember exactly when I realized that I AM consciousness and that I'm not just a body with a brain looking for my answers from somewhere outside of me.

As I began my spiritual path and realized that my true self is linked to everything else in the Universe at an energetic level, it definitely took the edge off my sense of righteousness.

I couldn't tell someone else what they should do any longer because I didn't know the true depth of the answer for myself anymore.

When I stepped out of my limited body-brain perception of myself and into considering myself as something much bigger, the power of diving into learning more about myself as a soul fascinated me. Expanding my inner knowing of who I truly am opened up a sense of oneness that I hadn't felt before.

The possibility that self-awareness is unlimited hit me hard. Many of the black and white answers that I had leaned on for years went away naturally, and questions became much more complex. And, to my delight, new colorful, perfectly formed answers emerged as I asked myself some truly powerful questions:

"What do I value now?"

"What do I believe about this now?"

"What matters to me now?"

Luckily, I listened to the answers (how couldn't I?) because they were more powerful than I'd ever experienced before. The answers

---

[42] Crystal Raypole, "Finding and Getting to Know Your Inner Child," Healthline. Last accessed Nov 2, 2021, https://www.healthline.com/health/inner-child#takeaway.

came from within, not only with such clarity but also with that powerful point-of no-return feeling in my body. There was truth present, and I felt it. And it was MY truth. That body sensation is how I knew I was on the right path. It was consciousness at play, linking me with my true self and sovereignty.

When we turn our gaze within for our "book of consciousness" that keeps gathering the chapters of our life every time we open our eyes, we can't go wrong. Our soul's story is being told as we go, with our original soul blueprint as a guide. Our answers may be different tomorrow than what they were yesterday, but what we experience today we didn't believe or know we could experience in the early chapters.

By living here, we're trying to get back to the essence of our true self, and that truth is found deep in our consciousness. This is what the adventure of self-awareness is. It's the power of knowing who we are at the soul level, not just what we prefer at the material level. No more listening to the small story within on what *should* be right for us in our ego's words or someone else's words. Our truth is within us at all times, and we have the opportunity to listen to the answers through our inner voice.

But most of the time, we're too busy or too enmeshed with our fearful ego to do that.

When we let go of the illusion of what has worked for others in the past and sit in the openness of our consciousness, that's when the answer emerges with such clarity and power that it can't be missed. And we don't even have to ask our best friend for advice anymore. Instead, we can share our own answers with our best friends in gratitude to our true selves.

Sounds too good to be true, right? No self-help books would be written if it were that easy... There's work involved.

To become a sovereign individual requires that we not only peel off the layers of family patterns and conditioning that have made up who we are so far but that we see ourselves and others differently.

We need to expose the core seed from which our soul was born, often in the form of our inner child, so that we can connect back with that pure core of our true self and get to know the playful limitlessness of it again.

I believe the inner calm comes with an inner knowing and belief that the lessons we learn throughout life can help us trust that every step we take is the right one.

With increased self-awareness, we get the opportunity to step into the feeling of living in our own truth and authenticity, aligned with our true selves, living through the heart and intuition with ease and flow.

But there's another thing...

Clearing Energy from the Past

Once we become sovereign and believe we deserve self-love, we feel self-empowered and motivated from within, (instead of through external validation). We're ready to grow, expand, and move forward to bring out all that we are here to give and experience in this life. But before we can hold our energy and sovereignty with ease, we are invited to clear the energy of our past patterns so that we can fully step into our sovereignty.

This way we create space within to invite the energy of our current values, inspiration, and sense of passion for life to not be held down by the past. The energetic work to release the past enables us to stay in the present and develop an inner support system and co-create with the Universe.

If we don't clear past energy attachments, we have a harder time moving on in a new way, so it's important to begin the work with clearing energy from the past as soon as possible.

Sometimes this energy clearing of the past never happens because self-love is still a lesson for us, but once we feel we deserve to grow at the soul level, it'll be evident that energy from the past needs to go.

The clearing of past energies can be done in different ways and at different levels. Simplified, energy clearing can be done through energy practices such as Reiki or acupuncture or a simple energy exercise you can do yourself to cut the emotional energetic cords from the past. You can even clean out your house, throw away old things, or burn sage; its smoke provides an immediate energy clearing of the space.

However, clearing of your inner energy more deeply often starts with acceptance and a process to detangle the connections of things, relationships, and the energies of the past so that a bigger picture can emerge.

When you get distance and perspective of past energies, it allows for release so that the space that's created can be filled with new energy for the future.

Once we clear ourselves from past energies, our aura becomes clear and strong. We are held up by our aura as we walk through life. When we're in our natural energy without distractions or interference, we strengthen our aura and attract good and healthy things into our lives. We stay focused and present and we are aware of synchronicities and divine timing.

Our heart is connected and open, and if we get off track, we know how to easily get back to heart-centered grounding and flow.

As a sovereign individual, you intuitively know what you need to do to get back in alignment with your natural energy, whether it's a slow walk or a few minutes of free-dancing to your favorite tune that does the trick.

All of this is possible if you begin to get curious about yourself and what you can learn just by believing that there IS, in fact, more to life than what you have now today. Everyone can grow from where they are today and become sovereign.

There is no completion in being you.

Exercise: Your Sovereign Self

Part I: Identify Codependency

In this exercise, you'll explore your behaviors of co-dependency. These questions have been adapted from Mental Health America's Codependency page.[43] Answer the questions below in your journal.

* Do you keep quiet to avoid arguments?
* Are you always worried about others' opinions of you?
* Are the opinions of others more important than your own?
* Do you doubt your ability to be who you want to be?
* Are you uncomfortable expressing your true feelings to others?
* Do you think people in your life would go downhill without your constant efforts?
* Do you frequently wish someone could help you get things done?
* Do you have trouble asking for help?

What can you learn from your answers?

Part II: Inner Child Conversation

How can you deepen your experience and connection to your inner child and creativity? This is a brief exercise using Lucia Capacchione's method to demonstrate that you, can contact and have a two-way written conversation between your adult self and your inner child.

Take out two pens and a piece of paper. Your non-dominant hand will represent your inner child, and your dominant hand will represent your adult self.

---

[43] Mental Health America, "Co-Dependency," Last accessed Nov 2, 2021, https://www.mhanational.org/co-dependency.

Ask your inner child, and with your dominant hand write down the question: "What do you need?"

Respond to this question with your non-dominant hand, writing down the answer. (Writing with your non-dominant hand will likely look like a child wrote it!)

Ask the next question that you want to ask your inner child and then the next, following the same structure until you want to conclude the conversation.

Part III: Viewing Yourself as Sovereign

Sovereignty is a personal breakthrough where you find yourself filled up with your inner power, self-love and motivation from within rather than seeking validation and energy from someone else or a situation.

How can you strengthen your sense of sovereignty?

* Maybe it's an experience of solitude after being in a relationship for a long time?
* Maybe it's a decision made only by you from start to finish?
* Maybe it's deciding to pick up a hobby or interest that you've been thinking about doing for a long time but have never gotten around to?
* Maybe it's setting up a meditation space in your home that is only for you?
* Maybe it's a day to yourself intentionally and regularly?

Whatever you decide to do to show yourself that you matter in your own life will support you in strengthening your sense of sovereignty.

Part IV: Energetic Clearing to Free Yourself

We carry energetic cords from the past unless we intentionally identify and cut them off. Our free will allows us to ask past energy to be released. With this simple exercise, you can perform an energy clearing.

First, it's important to identify what energy chords you are carrying. This can be done through an energy healer or working with the Akashic Records, but it can also be as simple as identifying emotional resistance to certain situations and relationships you may have.

Cutting cords by visualization is a simple and effective way to clear energy.

Visualize the cord between you and another person or situation. In your mind's eye, notice the quality of the cord and decide to cut it off with an imagined tool of your choice. Visualize yourself cutting it off and see the cord falling to the floor. Notice how you feel. You can repeat this exercise as often as you feel it's needed.

15

Shift 4: From Learning to Embodying

> *"You are the universe expressing itself as a human for a little while."*
> — Eckart Tolle

A client of mine, Rachel, wanted to feel less stress and pressure on herself. Her days were already filled with commitments, so she wondered, *How can I even find time to start something new?* Rachel shared with me that she had health and sleep issues and she was annoyed because they held her back from what she wanted to accomplish.

I asked her, "How willing are you to truly make a change?"

"Oh, I'm SO ready," she said, but when I asked her to find three things that she could let go of and not do, she couldn't identify anything to let go of. "They all have to be done," she said.

Rachel went on to describe her very tight daily schedule hour by hour (and sometimes down to the minute) to me, and it was evident that she had not a single minute of flexibility in her day. As a child, her schedule had been minutely planned for her, and she continued this pattern as an adult. The only way she knew how to get through a day was to have it planned out in detail.

No wonder she couldn't find anything to let go of. Her schedule dictated every single minute of her day. All things were a top priority!

I suggested letting go of the hourly scheduled tasks and instead introduced the concept of having three goals for the day. "What? I can't skip the schedule," she said. "It's my way of knowing what to do."

I said, "How motivated are you to feel less stressed?"

"I am SO motivated."

"OK, would you be willing to try this for at least a week?" I asked.

"Alright, a week can't hurt," she said.

As homework I asked her to come up with three goals for the next day that she wanted to accomplish. The following day, she came back with three goals. She said, "I want to have this report finalized and sent off to my boss, I want to have completed my research for the next project by tomorrow, and I want to have worked out at the gym."

The next day, off she went to try this new concept of focusing on the three goals instead of her fully packed daily calendar with millions of details. The next day, she called me and said, "I totally got distracted yesterday. So many unexpected things came up, and I got lost in that. I had to scramble at the end of the day to complete my three goals."

"What happened?" I asked. To only have goals and not tasks in a day threw her off. When we talked about why this happened, she became aware that she didn't know how to make decisions on her own when it came to where she put her energy.

Distraction is associated with spending energy, so when we are distracted, that energy is not staying within us. It's spent on the distraction itself, so we feel tired afterward.

When we get distracted, we are not experiencing our reality for a moment. The importance of inner transparency between ourselves and what is going on in our reality is key to staying in energetic flow.

Rachel and I worked on this new concept of broader goals and not having a minute-by-minute structure for a few weeks together with success. She had to reconsider her pattern of planning to the detail to discover what approach TRULY worked for her.

Then she could invite goals that were truly aligned with her own energy that created less stress and facilitated ease and flow in her day. She applied an important shift to her real life and saw a significant reduction in her inner stress levels and an increase in trust in herself.

Integration Through Taking Action

Our transformation beyond our current reality starts with the integration of what we learn about ourselves and the Universe into our experience from a multitude of perspectives. This will be different for each person depending on each person's path to authenticity and self-expression.

Essentially, taking action, motivated from within, towards a future that is *different* from our reality today is where the deep connection with our inner power and our true self and embodiment starts.

However, this is when our commitment to step out of the comfort zone is tested. Many people continue to stay stuck because they, for various reasons, stay in the comfort zone of learning more and more, instead of integrating and applying the learning. As Barbara Nordstrom Loeb says: "We privilege our thoughts and minds, without being curious about their relationship to the rest of who we are. Doing this, we end up feeling out of balance with our community, our world, and ourselves."[44]

Also, the sensation of sovereignty needs to be present so that others such as family, friends, or colleagues make us question our direction and talk us out of taking action on what we know through increased self-awareness is our truth.

If that intentional action or step forward is inspired by the love of what our hearts want, we are creating a flow of energy for ourselves. This step forward will look different for everyone, but it's an inner journey of courage and action.

There is no stopping now.

However, there is a big difference between igniting motivation and learning new perspectives about how to connect with our true selves and actually living it.

To live from your heart and intuition is to embody your true self.

---

[44] Barbara Nordstrom-Loeb, "Embodiment – How to Get It and Why It Is Important," Earl E. Bakken Center for Spirituality & Healing, University of Minnesota, Last accessed Nov 2, 2021, https://www.csh.umn.edu/news-events/blog/thoughts-about-embodiment-how-get-it-and-why-it-important.

Embodiment Is to Experience

According to the Oxford Dictionary, embodying means "to be an expression of or give a tangible or visible form to (an idea, quality, or feeling)."

I always believed that if I put my mind to it, I could learn whatever I needed to do next. And if there was something that I didn't know, I would look it up or watch someone do it to learn it, and then repeat it myself, and so on.

Naturally, I turned to what was easy for me. Through my spiritual growth journey I read books, many, many books by very wise, highly evolved spiritual teachers.

The stories, teachings, and practices were all very mind-opening, but that's exactly that — *mind* opening but not heart opening. Why is that? Through, for example, reading books we experience *someone else's* story or an experience of *their* insight and truth through *their* words and perspective as captured by the mind.

And that is all good. But in my experience, there's rarely a direct translation from someone else's perspective, experience, or teaching in a book, a course, or another event to my life experience. We can choose to put a book on the bookshelf after having read it, right? And our knowledge stays in the mind.

Heart opening and embodiment happen because of our *inner* experience and can only happen by actually *going through* the transformation of it.

To evolve from learning about the expanded experience we desire to embody it is a critical shift that defines the success of the rest of our soul's path. Embodying our desired change from within ourselves and living in alignment with our own energy, purpose, and rhythm is what matters on the path of soul growth, not how it looks on the outside to someone else, or what is created by us in physical form. It is how we feel emotionally and mentally (i.e., what frequency of vibration we spend our time in) that matters, and only we know the inner beauty of that.

What you may notice is the change in your aura, your self-expression, and your inner power. All of this shifts when you start living from your inner power and truth in connection with the Universe, instead of through validation by others.

Others can notice the change and difference in your belief in yourself and what matters to you. As mentioned before, these can be changes in your diet, or what you want to spend time on, getting into new hobbies or activities that you never have been interested in before, and so on.

You may or may not have noticed this shift in yourself yet. You will know deep within that you've opened the door to your inner creativity and abundance that is so rich that you'd never want to go back to anything else. You can't miss it!

Inner Transparency

This shift from learning to embodying is all about taking action and following our inner spark, inner power, and inner guidance even more. But this can't happen unless we show ourselves the inner transparency of taking action from a place of balance between our inner and outer expression. If we don't have inner transparency, we can't go deeper to trust our heart and intuition fully.

If there's inner transparency between who we are outward with who we are inward, we can begin to embody our true self under the guidance of our inner voice and not our ego mind. In an article by Jorge N. Ferrer titled "What Does it Mean to Live a Fully Embodied Spiritual Life?", the author claims that it's crucial to stay connected to our body and nature to stay in our reality of our truth and "develop fully as human beings without needing to 'escape' anywhere to find our essential identity and feel whole,"[45] whether that is escapism through consistent learning, addictions, or illusions of self-importance.

When I was struggling every day, I didn't even understand what inner transparency between my body, mind, heart, and soul energies was, and therefore, I had no aligned sensation of what was needed for my own energy flow to stay in balance. Instead, a feeling of resistance was present within me daily.

Inner transparency is when we feel that our inner voice and body consciousness are working together. The ego mind is not interested in putting the two together because when it happens, we gain clarity

---

[45] Jorge N. Ferrer, "What Does It Mean to Live A Fully Embodied Life?," *International Journal of Transpersonal Studies* 27 (2008): 1-11.

about how we give our power away. But our heart knows that's how we find peace.

The opportunity for you is to have inner transparency to stay in energetic flow. The more you practice inner transparency with yourself, the more you get clear about your reality and what is cluttering your energy flow.

In what area of life do you feel imbalanced between your inner and outer perception? Is it in a relationship that is draining you or how you show up at home versus with friends?

When we apply inner transparency and can clearly see what's making us resist our own needs for balance, or what's keeping the fire hose of energy welling out of us as we give our power away, we are more likely to be able to pull back to stay in energetic flow and alignment with ourselves and our environment; we have a greater chance of being able to turn the knob to stop the outgoing overflow.

As you learn how to walk through life with inner transparency, gone is the self-doubt and procrastination and the negative self-talk that the mind engages in. Instead, it's a feeling of knowing the next step already, before it's even there.

The Shift from Learning to Embodying

I used to be this fast-moving super mom with her work bag, diaper bag, and purse on her shoulder backing the car out the garage in the morning. On the surface, I lived an organized and successful life, but I also lived on shallow emotions due to sheer speed. When I shifted within, my outer expression had to change too.

The outer change has been noticeable. I move much more slowly in life now. I prefer to do fewer things at once and I prefer to take breaks during the day to look up to the sky and to connect to what's going on within. I am not into matching clothes or wearing makeup to the extent I was before. I don't worry about how others see me.

Now I feel confident in social situations because I trust my inner voice and body wisdom to signal to me what hasn't been saying and what I cannot see. I tap into my wisdom. The wholeness and embodiment of my true self have become who I am now.

It's a transformation that lasts.

In addition, our external environment and the people in it may change, or stay the same, depending on how they align with our transformation, or don't. People who grow at a similar pace meet us where we are now. It may be difficult to accept that people we have considered close to us in the past no longer feel like they are on the same wavelength. Staying in relationships that are no longer aligned with the way we approach life now is only going to delay our path forward.

This can be especially frustrating between partners when one is evolving at a faster pace than another, and our ability to relate with compassion and forgiveness is paramount in situations like that.

As stated in an article in HackSpirit, "Unless you are blessed with very open-minded people in your life, the heart-sinking experience of watching your loved one's zone out as you explain your newfound spiritual knowledge will inevitably take place"[46]

As we continue to explore these shifts, we want to ensure that we can continue to follow through. Our ego might want us to revert back to the comfort zone and not expand these shifts "too much." This is natural, but if that happens, we must go back to that "point of no return feeling." That inner feeling helps us to not look back, only expand forward even more.

Our natural transformational energy of evolution will find its way to full expression no matter what. Whenever we are expressing ourselves fully, we see only beauty. When the wheel of transformation is turning in your favor, your empowerment cannot be stopped.

Even if we are conditioned to believe that our circumstances are caused by others, we *can* keep going, no matter what is happening or who is around us, unless we allow it to slow down or stop. We are now the ones keeping the momentum of our own transformation. There is no one else to thank. We are in the driver's seat.

Once you start to believe that you can have all that beauty and abundance sourced from within you and allow it to be felt in your heart, there is no stopping you!

[46] Kiran Athar, "11 Signs of a Spiritual Awakening Ending Your Relationship," HackSpirit, Last accessed Nov 2, 2021, https://hackspirit.com/spiritual-awakenings-ending-your-relationship/.

Exercise:
Embodiment Reality Check!

"OK, what's the situation, really?"

That's a good question to ask yourself. Inner transparency is your perception of yourself on the inside and your perception of who you are on the outside. If there is too much difference in our perception of our reality today and who we want to be, resistance and self-doubt are created.

When you get real about what's going on right now, the opportunity to change the situation is right in front of you.

In that moment, decide if you're going to complain about how stressful your workday is so far OR if you're going to look for what's good about the day so far?

I'd like to challenge you to stretch yourself. Prove to yourself there is something good in ANY situation. By bringing in a thought of gratitude, you'll give yourself the positive boost you need on a stressful day.

One of the first steps to come to inner transparency is to observe your current reality.

Part I: What is your reality today?

You can observe your current situation with a simple meditation:

I recommend allowing at least a 10-minute timed meditation where you invite yourself to observe yourself from the outside. Through your inner vision, follow yourself at work, with the kids, and with family and friends. Just observe. No judgment, no solutions; just walk beside yourself and notice. Notice how you move. What are your facial expressions? How do you interact with others? Notice your body language.

Immediately after the meditation, journal about what you noticed about yourself. Write down what comes up with no edits. Just the way it is. As if you were describing someone with objective eyes.

This is your reality.

The next step is to write out the feelings you have inside of yourself about this image. Honor your feelings and how you describe them.

The transparency we're trying to unearth is how we can align the perception of yourself that you want to come across as with your inner feelings of your reality.

Part II: Who do you want to be?

Next comes a clear vision of who you want to become.

Set your timer for another 10-minute meditation, visualizing yourself as you want to be.

Take yourself on a walk, somewhere of your choice, and just observe. No judgement, no solutions; just walk beside yourself and notice. Notice how you move. What are your facial expressions? How do you interact with others? Notice your body language.

Immediately after the meditation, journal on a new page about what you notice about yourself and who you want to be.

The next step is to write out the feelings you have inside yourself related to who you want to be. Believe your feelings and how you describe them.

Then, the most important part is to notice the difference between how you describe and feel about your reality today and who you want to be.

Why are there differences (if any)? How can you accept these differences? Or how can you start working on aligning these perceptions? How can you work towards embodying who you want to be?

Part III: Embody with Dance

It sounds simple, but one of the most effective ways to embody who you want to be is through dance. There are very few things that bring your whole being to its full expression like dancing without restriction to your favorite tune.

Bring in a vision of what you worked on in the exercise above and become it!

16

Shift 5: From Logic to Wisdom

> *"You don't always need a plan. Sometimes*
> *you just need to breathe, let go and see what happens"*
> — Mandy Hale.

T he rain was coming down heavy outside. I was sitting in my kitchen, thinking to myself, *Why do things happen the way they do?* This morning I had started my workday at 5:30 a.m. I went right to my computer before the kids woke up, sitting at my desk in my robe and fuzzy slippers. There was just that one email that had to be taken care of first thing in the morning.

And now it was already evening. The day had turned into night, and I was still in work-mode, answering emails and filling out forms for the next thing that needed to go out the next day.

Where did the day go? I couldn't even remember the details of the day—what my kids had shared with me over dinner, or the story my husband told me about how he found a part to his dive gear that he had been looking for online for so long.

All I could focus on was how tired I was.

I didn't see that the struggle I experienced was supposed to be experienced in that moment. And that moment is perfect. Because a moment of struggle is showing us where we can grow further.

Now I believe that struggle is perfect!

But I didn't always see struggle as perfect. In the past, I saw struggle as something I needed to get rid of as fast as possible. By working even harder, focusing even more, and trying to figure things out.

I was relentless in keeping my mind focused on a single task, and I didn't stop until the work was done. There were days when I hadn't had lunch and only a five-minute break to eat dinner after cooking and serving the rest of the family.

My way of approaching my day with logic and "the way it was supposed to be" resulted in struggle, which I tried to get out of with more struggle. I can't even clearly remember how I managed to operate that way for such a long time.

The work just had to be done, no matter what. Ten extra minutes were precious. Many emails could be fired off in ten minutes while taking a phone call while figuring out the next step back then, believe me.

I didn't have the feeling that a bigger plan was at play at all because my entire being felt the struggle with getting a breakthrough at work after many months of non-stop go.

Life didn't feel effortless at all.

But my soul wanted life to be effortless.

So what happened?

How could I go from treating struggle as a punching bag to treating struggle as a perfectly white cloud floating by?

I let the grip around my bow and arrow loosen. I put down the boxing gloves. I let the need for control go. I abandoned the idea that I always had to have the answers available. I let struggle and resistance flow through me instead of absorbing it.

I aligned with my own energy instead of working against it. Feelings are energy. When we avoid connecting with our true feelings, we avoid the flow of our energy, so the more we have feelings of resistance, the more we work against our own energy.

As I started to see my struggles as blessings and opportunities to show me where I could grow, I saw how my struggle was trying to tell me something.

Let Go of the Ego's Rules

The struggle we're experiencing comes with a clue. Struggle is like an energetic knot that wants to be untied and released.

For me, approaching my day with a perception of always having to struggle was a way to procrastinate in other areas of life.

It was a way to deal with an overwhelming demand for my time and attention, for example, in family and work life. I was keeping busy multitasking just to move life comfortably ahead, day after day, week after week, year after year.

The busy hustle culture we have praised for so long turns out to be a big fat off switch to any kind of opportunity to get out of the comfort zone. Most importantly, the off switch is a way to keep life shallow and on the emotional surface.

As the opportunity turned up to "flip the switch" and to go deeper to reconnect with what my passions were, the inner voice of my true self, my inner world, became stronger and more prominent than the demands of the external world, such as caving in to the logic needed to solve most work tasks.

Now I know that things happen in the perfect way with no struggle required. It's just the way it's supposed to be. Life can progress effortlessly if we allow it to. When we allow our day to run effortlessly and in flow, there's space and stillness created within for wisdom to enter, while the busy-bee mentality becomes less and less appealing.

When we're ready to go deeper and stop using the energy of struggle as a default to approach our everyday life, we begin to trust. When we trust, we invite our heart energy, our intuition, and body wisdom to help us with how we perceive our day, and we can truly make a permanent shift within.

The core of this shift is happening when we let go of following the rules we don't resonate with anymore and when we stop relying on step-by-step instructions that we're supposed to follow to be successful. This shift happens when we stop relying on our ego's stories and start noticing out-of-the-blue signs, synchronicities, instant intuitive hits, and immediate body sensations in all life situations.

By making this shift, we build trust in our inner knowing and we learn how to set and manage our energetic boundaries. We go from relying on the logic that the mind conjures up based on knowledge to instead listening to and experiencing our own wisdom.

Detaching the Thinking, Logical Mind

When I told my ego mind's voice that I was done listening to it, everything changed. I had found access to a complete, new, unlimited dimension in my true self where my wisdom was readily available, without the mind always being involved.

One of the reasons for not feeling joyful is that we're letting the ego get in the way of our potential to live our best life every day.

The mind makes up assumptions about our lives. We then put those assumptions on repeat constantly; we believe that those assumptions are true without questioning them.

The logical mind is driven by the ego, and often the ego is diverting us away from present joy by keeping us in the past and future. The ego wants us to stay where we are, think of everything that could go wrong, and not go beyond what we know; it wants us to just play safe.

According to a LifeHack article, knowledge is about facts and ideas that we acquire through study, research, investigation, observation, or experience. Wisdom is the ability to discern and judge which aspects of that knowledge are true, right, lasting, and applicable to your life.[47]

With this expansion of perception I had to let go of some outdated beliefs about the use and importance of my mind and the role it had played in my life up until now.

The mind keeps us thinking, and thinking, and thinking. The body helps us express ourselves in the physical world.

When we are not driven by the mind anymore, and instead are aligned with our heart and intuition, we allow our true selves to guide our actions. It's effortless. Things just happen. The trust we have for ourselves and that our actions are the right ones makes it feel like it's not a huge risk to take action. It doesn't feel like we have to struggle and invest a huge effort or prepare for months beforehand. The planning and worry that the logical mind comes up with can hinder us in proceeding to the next best step because we can't see the path forward for all the "what-if" scenarios that are made up by the mind. When we are living from the heart and intuition, we can sense the next step and trust that it's the right move forward.

Things that are created as a result of being connected with the wisdom of our true selves just come into form naturally—at least, that's how it seems—and flow in harmony with our own energy and the energy of the universe.

There is a different level of courage in creating something physical, instead of continuing to create in the mind and never taking action on it.

---

[47] Royale Scuderi, "What Are the Differences Between Knowledge, Wisdom, and Insight?," Lifehack, https://www.lifehack.org/articles/communication/what-are-the-differences-between-knowledge-wisdom-and-insight.html.

We are embodying this alignment with our life purpose into physical form without hesitation or doubt because it's in direct connection with our true self.

If we feel we have to take a risk, take a leap, or we feel something is a huge effort, that perception is generated by the mind, where all doubt is generated.

This shift from logic to wisdom teaches us to detach from the mind's games of the past and future and be present here and now to receive the right next action through our true self's inner voice and body sensations in the moment.

Integrate Your Body Wisdom

As discussed in Chapter 10, we can experience our body's wisdom through intentional movements such as yoga, intuitive dance, spontaneous laughing, mantra, and breathwork. The intention behind it is to become more aware of what the body is telling us, sharing its ancient wisdom captured from past lifetimes and generations.

As we shift from living from a reference of logic to wisdom, we become more and more curious about not only what the message from the body is in certain situations but also what it means. To integrate the body's wisdom and live with that source of information daily means to interpret and take action upon the body's messages in light of what is going on in our lives right now, even if it's beyond logical reason or mental hypothesis.

This may mean that you sense something in your body that needs to be checked out, even if you don't have any symptoms, or intuitively know what remedy to use when feeling under the weather, trusting that it's the right approach.

It can also mean that you are naturally awakening your innate, unique abilities as a healer not only for self-healing but for your family and others.

When we live intuitively with our body's wisdom, we live through our bodies' experiences, not our minds. Moreover, our intuitive abilities and third eye energy center, located between the eyebrows, are connected to the heart, not the mind. Experiencing life from the perspective of the body's wisdom and sensations will be important as we connect more and more with our true selves.

A Shift to Unity Consciousness

As a child, at around nine or ten years old, I believed that my grandmother who had passed away was with me and she was able to talk to me from Heaven because that's where I was told people went when they died. As a child, I prayed to her, asking for things or letting her know when I really wanted something to happen.

Many of us have had childhood experiences like that. We see consciousness and the spirit world as something *separate* from our physical selves that we can ask for things from and hope for a speedy delivery.

For some this perception of separation remains into adulthood, and for some of us, the perception of consciousness merges into an experience of unity where there is no separation between the Universal consciousness and the consciousness of ourselves. I believe this is what the experience of our true selves is. An experience of union of our true self and Universal consciousness where we see the true self as part of the Universal consciousness and therefore see it as unlimited.

Unity consciousness can be simply defined as "thinking and ultimately acting in ways that unite us to ourselves, others, Nature or to the God of our own understanding"[48] So if our true selves and Universal consciousness are perceived to be the same through the perspective of the heart, why don't we always connect to this union for the answers we're seeking? That is a good question, but my simple suggestion is that until now we have believed that this union and connection with the Universe has been reachable only for a sacred few and not available to everyone. But, in reality, it is available to you now!

In Charge of Our Energy

Our energy extends way beyond our physical bodies. Our energy fields are vibrational frequencies resulting from our thoughts and beliefs and our bodies' capacities to hold energy at a certain level. It's our energy fields that other people interact with.

You've probably heard "it starts with me," and it truly does. You are in charge of your energy field (aura) and your own energy exchange with others. That's why it's so important to know more

---

[48] Paul Dunion, "Unity Consciousness," Huffpost, Last accessed Nov 2, 2021, https://www.huffpost.com/entry/unity-consciousness_b_8244982.

about your own natural energy—to be able to expand on the energy that is natural to you.

Our energy field is also dependent on those we surround ourselves with. So, as important as it is to do our inner work and hold our own energy frequency at all times, it is also important to be aware of who we surround ourselves with and their energy fields.

For example, if we let others determine what's right for us, we take on and embody their energy fields. Most likely, it's not an exact match to our natural energy, and we feel off.

This awareness is key to understanding more about how our relationships impact us and how we allow (or do not allow) this energy exchange to happen. Donna Eden, in her book *Energy Medicine*, says, "Your energies are, in fact, so distinctive, and they so potently regulate your physical body, that you begin to look like your energy body just as surely as two people who share a life for fifty years sometimes begin to resemble each other."[49]

Interestingly, this interplay can all happen without words. The body's (and heart's) wisdom knows and senses someone else's energy field when we are simply in their presence. But we are so conditioned to judge others by appearance and their words and actions that we often ignore the body sensations when we meet someone.

The body can sense if we're attached to or have aligned with an energy that is not serving us. If we have attached to someone else's lower energy, the body can identify it, usually before the mind does. We may not be able to put words to it at the time, as the mind often comes up with reasons to ignore an energetic body sensation and focus on something else or ignore it.

Sometimes we may be in a situation and notice that we're suddenly not behaving at our best. We wonder, *Why is this happening?* It could be that we've aligned with someone else's energy without knowing it. But the body intuitively knows.

When we become open to believing that our body is a different tool for learning and guidance than what we have used it for previously (i.e., not just to carry out what the mind comes up with), we can also tap into our true self's inner voice, which is always our truth, much

---

[49] Donna Eden and David Feinstein, *Energy Medicine: Balancing Your Body's Energies for Optimal Health, Joy, and Vitality* (Los Angeles: Jeremy P. Tarcher, 2008).

easier. The shift can happen when we become aware that we have attached to energy that is not our own.

We may also notice repeat situations where we react in the same negative way. Once we notice it, it becomes easier to let go of and shift repeating patterns that are holding us in a lower energy pattern.

In addition, the Universe is helping us highlight these moments of opportunity for shifts through synchronicities. Synchronicities are patterns or symbols that repeat themselves to help us see what we need to see and that help guide us to see where we have an opportunity to shift. The wisdom we bring to this lifetime is deeply imprinted in us already, but as long as we keep ourselves away from connecting with the wisdom hosted within our hearts and our bodies, we will resort to logic as the truth.

This is your opportunity to make a shift and expand yourself beyond the perspective of logic and the physical and live in concert with the unlimited potential of the Universe.

Exercise:
Your Soul's Wisdom Unlimited

Part I: Past Life Connection

This meditation is designed to broaden your perspective of your soul's life. You can ask someone to guide you or record yourself reading it on your phone and then experience it. Find a comfortable seat and close your eyes. Imagine you are standing on a beach. You can see the horizon and the sky above. There is an island on the horizon. It is far away, but you know deep down that you have been there before.

A magical bridge appears between where you are standing and the island. You begin to walk over the bridge. You feel held and supported as you walk.

You arrive at the island.

What do you see? You may appear as another person on the outside, but it's you. Begin with noticing your clothes, your shoes. Notice the detail.

Next, look around. What do you see?

Spend some time here on the island. When you feel ready to return over the magical bridge, do so.

Part II: Tap Into Your Heart Joy

Let your heart lead your actions today! What does this leading with your heart really mean? When we connect with the joy that's already within us, it's not because we carefully planned it; it's because we are in a state of alignment, creativity, spontaneity, and freedom. All of these qualities are qualities of the heart.

In this exercise, you'll tap into the wisdom of your heart (instead of your logic). Feel the difference!

1. Think about a situation where you experienced something for the first time and instantaneously a new sensation was born within you that you had never felt before.

The sense of wonder and awe we get from experiences like that are connected to the heart. They can't be planned out in advance; they just happen naturally.

2. The second thing to do if you want to connect back to a state of joy is to envision yourself being in the state of joy using a select memory from the past that was particularly joyful. You can put yourself in that energy right now!

Part III: Let's Connect to the Joy in Your Life

Take out your journal and explore these questions:

*   When was the last time you had the time of your life?
*   What were some of the feelings that you felt?
*   What was the situation? Who was around you? Where were you?

Describe this event in detail or draw a colorful picture. Connect back to this moment of joy right now.

Your job is to immerse yourself in the feeling of this past joyful situation. Bring this vision and feeling of joy into a meditation. I bet once you do, you'll be smiling already!

See! Joy is already there inside you!

You have access to it. You just have to connect your heart to it before your mind tells you something else...

What can you DO differently in your life today that will bring forward that feeling of joy in your life again?

17

Shift 6: From Pushing to Manifesting

> *"When you shift to this higher energy and resonate more in harmony with intention, you become a magnet for attracting more of this energy into your world."*
> — Wayne Dyer

I've always had a strong need to feel financially secure, which was expressed through my strong focus on career. This need to feel financially secure diverted me from my true needs of freedom, creativity, and self-empowerment. I focused on my reality every day in a short-term manner. I was doing, doing, doing so that someday I'd be able to get to a point where I didn't have to push so hard to create what I wanted.

My focus was pretty much one week at a time, just to make sure the wheels were turning and things were moving forward in the right direction. I focused on my reality every day and I complained and stressed about it—to myself mostly. The inner dialogue was harsh and unforgiving.

At that time, I never got to the point of allowing myself to truly stretch my imagination into what I truly wanted next. I believed that since my reality was full of stress and deadlines, my future would also be full of stress, unless I worked harder to get ahead.

A few years ago, I set an intention to transition from my long-term career into my life's work as a life coach. I infused that intention into a crystal bracelet that I had created while visualizing my dream scenario.

First, after a centering meditation I cleared any mind-created limitations with a powerful kundalini mantra. Then, I called on my dream. I started to visualize what I wanted to welcome into my life.

I totally let my wildest dreams come to life, with no limitations, what-ifs, or buts.

After a few minutes of living my dream through a vision, I closed up my bracelet. I put it on my wrist and wore it every day, and every day, I felt the power of being reminded of my intention and what I was welcoming into my life. The reminder of my intention has made all the difference.

My intention hasn't faded, it hasn't gone away, and it hasn't changed. It is as alive as it was the day I set the intention, thanks to the reminder the bracelet constantly gave me.

I am proud to say that two years after I set the intention, wearing my bracelet every day for those two years, I made the career shift that I wanted.

I was in awe.

Meeting Our Needs

As a life coach I work with people who want their realities to be different. Ultimately, this is because they believe their needs are not met. Some believe nothing is going their way.

When we want to change but nothing is happening, or so it seems, it may be that we've lost connection with what is here and now.

The moment you're reading this is your reality. It's the only moment you can just be; otherwise, you're either in the past or in the future. So, in reality, your needs are met in this moment because you are here. And the here and now is not supposed to be changed; it's not supposed to be pushed into something different. Believe it or not, when we're in the flow of what is, all of our needs are met.

The work is initially about transforming the *belief* around what our needs are and how well they are met today as we fully step into who and what we are here to be and to make decisions that are right for us.

In other words, what we believe we need today can be changed into something completely different tomorrow. When our needs change, we change. In addition, manifestation is not only about beliefs. As reported by Psychology Today, science suggests that our beliefs bring about behaviors (and responses from others) that lead to the outcomes we desire.[50]

This is where the manifestation lies.

Using Our Intuition

By staying connected to our intuition we allow ourselves to relate to a higher perspective and truths beyond what we can see and touch. The energy frequency and vibration of the heart is a better match to receive transmission from our true self than the energy of our logical mind.

I believe that when we're connected to our intuition, our mind functions as a screen that projects messages from our true self via our third eye to our heart. When this happens, we can choose to trust those messages from our true selves, felt by our hearts and bodies. As Jack Canfield says, "The Universe rewards those who take action—and so does your intuition. When you act on the information you receive from your inner source of wisdom, you open the channel between your subconscious and conscious mind even wider and will receive more intuitive messages that are stronger and easier for you to hear and act on."[51]

We're starting to realize that manifestation is actually less about the thoughts of our mind and more about our inner energy, especially the heart energy and our ability to trust, believe, and act on our intentions, intuitive hits, signs, and synchronicities to point us in the direction of what we want to manifest.

The Awareness of Passion and Self-Love

As adults we have the opportunity to align with the passion of effortless manifestation, which is fueled by the energy of unconditional self-love that comes from who we are as a soul, our true self.

---

[50] Tchiki Davis, "What Is Manifestation? Science-Based Ways to Manifest," Psychology Today. Last accessed Nov 2, 2021. https://www.psychologytoday.com/ca/blog/click-here-happiness/202009/what-is-manifestation-science-based-ways-manifest.

[51] "7 Tips to Strengthen Your Intuition and Take Soul-Inspired Action," Jack Canfield, Last accessed Nov 2, 2021. https://www.jackcanfield.com/blog/cultivating-intuition/.

Personally, in the past, I didn't understand what self-love was, and I didn't know how to receive and reward myself from within, so I put my focus on something external that could give me the sensation of inner passion and reward to feel good about myself.

I call this *conditional* passion, and the reason for that is that I didn't include myself as a possible source of passion. I only included what others were able to give me, or the satisfaction that I gained through my career and what I was able to receive within the defined framework of rewards.

What I didn't realize at the time was that the passion I felt for my work was spoon-fed to me in a conditional way. If I performed well, I got rewarded materially and I felt good about myself. This pattern became a passion of mine as a substitute for sourcing my own self-love.

I had to learn how to give myself unconditional self-love. How did I do it? Learning how to tap into and trust my true self and my inner voice enabled me to turn the search for the passion-reward energy pattern away from work and instead start to focus on honoring and including my own needs as part of how to feel good about myself.

Unconditional self-love can only be given to us from ourselves; everything else is conditional self-love. When we're self-sufficient in expressing unconditional self-love within ourselves, we feel self-worth. When we are filled with the sensation of self-worth, we manifest effortlessly.

This is an internal energy loop that has nothing to do with anyone else, the past, or a circumstance in the present. It doesn't matter how much external reward we are able to accumulate through a conditional passion (such as work); we still don't feel true self-worth.

This is a fundamental lesson that many of us have had to go through, or are still going through, as adults as part of soul growth. When the energy of self-worth is completely sourced internally, it's also one of the enablers of unconditional passion. Having love and compassion for yourself isn't selfish, and according to an article from Positive Psychology, it's "actually a great way to make sure you're doing the best you can and impacting others positively."[52]

The passion I know now is not dependent on anyone else or what I do. It's the universal power and passion that we all can connect to

---

[52] Courtney E. Ackerman, "What is Self-Compassion and What is Self-Love?," Positive Psychology, Last accessed Nov 2, 2021, https://positivepsychology. com/self-compassion-self-love/.

that embraces us unconditionally and is not connected to what we produce or accomplish.

Passion is a life force that is love in itself and is the source for where our self-expression is taking us next. Now, I feel passion from within myself when I am in my element, aligned with my own natural energy, in balance, naturally expressing my gifts and talents effortlessly.

Internally, this passion has the texture of peace, calm, and self-confidence because I now know what I'm here to contribute, and I trust myself in a completely new way irrespective of who I'm with or what I do (for work).

When I'm working with a client, I feel passion in the moment as I observe her having a breakthrough insight that simultaneously releases stagnant inner energy in a coaching conversation. I feel passion when I walk outside, putting my hand on a tree to communicate with it for a moment. Those are the moments of passion and reward for me now. Not the conditional passion experienced in the waiting game of a slight probability of someone mentioning that I did a good job, or putting in the extra hours to maybe secure that next promotion.

As mentioned above, the discovery of how self-love feels and the energy of self-love when it's present (and when it's not) is very much linked to passion. If passion is directed and focus is kept outwardly, as in my case towards a career, passion becomes conditional. But when passion is directed towards self, it becomes unconditional self-love. With that comes a change in inner conversation as well. Our inner voice changes when we feel that passion, self-worth, and inner life force bubbling up. We're no longer chasing passion as a moving target. The inner state of self-acceptance is when unconditional self-love is right here within us at all times, and it's not going anywhere. "It means that I accept myself as I am at this moment; I accept that I have limitations and flaws. I still want to learn and grow and improve, but I also accept who I am right now," as described in an article in PsychCentral.[53]

Our inner voice becomes a voice of truth, more laid back, softer, less demanding, flowing, loving, a continuous stream of encouraging

---

[53] Sharon Martin, "How I Transformed my Self-Criticism into Self-Love," PsychCentral, Last accessed Nov 2, 2021, https://psychcentral.com/blog/imperfect/2020/02/how-i-transformed-my-self-criticism-into-self-love#Transform-self-criticism-into-self-acceptance.

support of our own growth. It encourages us to evolve instead of applying pressure to exceed others' expectations in the next task set out before us. The inner voice becomes more curious, forgiving, and allowing because now the focus is on feeling good and maintaining inner and outer balance. This is vastly different from before—when the inner voice compared everything and everyone to our latest performance. Now it doesn't pay all that much attention to what others say or do because the greater desire is to detach from the opinions of others and harness the uniqueness of our creativity.

I love the inner voice of my true self. It's fueling my self-love. It's my passion now.

The Secret to Receiving

Every day I start with something I intend to accomplish that day. Often my calendar has things scheduled, but I know I'll get to it at some point, or I'll move it to another day. In my past, to move something to another day was unacceptable. I just HAD to do it that day. I wouldn't stop until it was done as planned. I would feel exhausted after a long virtual meeting with millions of slides. It was like I had released every ounce of energy into the soup of information and opinions, trying my best to move the conversation forward yet another day. I rarely listened to my inner voice, my mind was in overdrive, and with that I easily became defensive. There was very little feeling of reward or magical creation going on.

Now, the way I approach a day is that I let it loose. I let it go wherever it wants to go. I receive the energy of where it takes me instead of putting my will into it because as soon as I put my will to something, I work against the natural flow that surrounds the creation of the moment. It is a practice of deeply listening to where the moment wants to go.

I practice the receiving of energy in this way, especially during a coaching session with a client. I am focused on receiving the entire time, which allows me to coach the client to the exact question that needs to be asked at that point in the session. It feels like a reward. It doesn't feel like work. I come out of a coaching session energized!

Receiving is a loop of energy within us that is activated once we feel genuine self-love and gratitude for what and who we are, what we have, and where we are in life right now. The energy of receiving is the effortless flow of eternity, far from the energy of over-the-top performance, getting ahead, or driving towards a deadline with a finite reward.

As beautifully said by author Mia Fox, "Gratitude is helpful for manifesting because it creates a state of abundance within us and changes our mindset. By merely focusing on the things you are grateful for in your life creates an understanding that you are provided for, you are safe, and you have plenty."[54]

The secret to receiving is that it's the energy of reward ALL THE TIME. Even while we're working on it.

If we choose to see it that way.

To walk through life looking at ambition as if a gift that is given to me every day and realizing that I receive this gift constantly WITHOUT having to struggle—this has been one of my key life lessons.

What I've learned is that the reward offered to us at all times is called gratitude. Gratitude is an energy of inner reward at all times that exceeds any material gift, and we can call on it whenever we want, at any time of the day, no matter the circumstance. It's the ever-present energy of creation.

A new discovery for me was that this energy is associated with no effort, and at first, I wasn't sure I could just receive just like that. Without any pre-work or boxes ticked off first? *Really? Is that even possible?*

It is.

All those years, I pushed so hard to show others (and myself) that I qualified for a reward. I now realized that I could have given myself that gift right away.

Mind blown.

Receiving is about tapping into the inner voice of gratitude. When we do so, we create and receive effortlessly because when we allow ourselves to receive within the energy of gratitude, we also create effortlessly. And when we create effortlessly, we manifest.

This is a quality of creation that is aligned with what you're supposed to create, not based on what someone else has done or said you should, or what has been done before. This energy of reward is received within; you're not projecting the energy outwards. It's all for YOU to experience within.

---

[54] Mia Fox, "The Power of Gratitude For Manifesting," Self Made Ladies, Last accessed Nov 2, 2021, https://selfmadeladies.com/power-gratitude-manifesting/.

Staying in an energy of receiving is a way of taming your own ego mind and taming the ambition that puts you in the push-and-do energy. When you can energetically wait, hold off, and receive, it all happens. The reward is that you are manifesting effortlessly and just being at the same time.

Clues Through Synchronicities

When we learn to notice signs and synchronicities, we also learn to receive. It's the Universe saying, "Look here! There is something that is meant for you (if you want it)." It's this seed of inspiration that we can pick up and do something with if we so wish.

The good news is that these nuggets are specific to us and are placed out by the Universe for us to align with if we want to. When you're in tune with synchronicity, you're in the creative space, and action is effortless because it's fueled by an open gate of universal support.

Previously, I would realize much later that I had missed an opportunity or worse, the chance to act on it was long gone. But now, as a synchronicity is happening, I am completely aware that it's happening, thanks to being connected with my intuition. I can also decide to take action in the moment on it (like I did with the decision to enroll in the coaching training).

Being in the creative space is being in the energy of action at the same time. Creativity and the desire to act go together, so when we envision something we would like to welcome into our lives, we are creative, and action is right behind that creative spark.

By tapping into the energy of creativity, abundance, and passion at the same time, we're manifesting a new reality. As stated in the book *You Are the Universe* by Deepak Chopra and Means Kafatos, "All of us live in a participatory universe. Once you decide that you want to participate fully, with mind, body and soul, that paradigm shift becomes personal."[55] With creativity on board, moving on (and up!) becomes this exciting expansion of inner power, instead of the restrictive, pre-determined path of self-judgment to check the box of the next step.

---

[55] Deepak Chopra and Menas Kafatos, *You Are the Universe: Discovering Your Cosmic Self and Why It Matters* (New York City: Harmony, 2017).

So many times I've tried to make something happen just by strategically wanting it so bad. Without that synchronistic confirmation from the Universe of "Hey, look over here!" (sign), however, very little was happening, and I was left wondering why. If I saw some movement in what I believed was the right direction, it was after much struggle, and I was ready to give up at any moment.

The difference here is clear. Trying to create without that universal support can prove to be a downhill ride on a plastic bag along a narrow path of rocks. On the other hand, co-creation with the Universe is a flowing flight through a wide-open space with all kinds of pleasant surprises along the way.

Imagine being able to connect with the creative downloads, signs, and synchronicities that are presented to you. It's not something you see with your eyes. It can be a feeling that is presented to you, or an idea coming to you in a split second, but every time it happens, you know it it's specifically just for you, and you go with it, instead of applying your logic to it, which would immediately box it into something smaller than what it could be.

Imagine your intuition and body's inner knowing being on board and very present and alive in your life. It's a transformation that opens up the opportunity to not only create in union with the Universe but also provides increased self-confidence in what you share and put out in the world. It's like your creative antenna just needs to be up, and the Universe sends ideas for you to respond to.

It's a practice of staying open to our imagination working as a mirror to the universe and allowing ourselves to dream and not box ourselves in when it comes to pursuing something. There's nothing more beautiful than receiving universal energy through your inner voice.

Imagine how creativity could be present for you in a deeper way.

The Effects of Distraction

So, if you are struggling with feeling disconnected from what you want next, and therefore, resist action in taking the next step in life, what is the issue? It sounds so easy just to put up that antenna, and off we go, working with the Universe. Our creative genius comes alive to kick us into action. But it's not that easy. There's never one reason, obviously, but in my experience, for many, the issue is distraction, which means that our focus and energy is placed somewhere outside ourselves. And once the focus is outside ourselves, there's no connection with our intuition or inner voice.

Some are seeking guidance from their environment to help find the next best way, and they keep asking and asking. Often, it's a desire to escape an environment, situation, or relationship, and that often brings our energy to focus on the past or the future. Or it's a focus on a need that is not met, so we keep looking to fill that void from the outside world.

One thing is clear—there are no synchronicities to be found in the past or the future. Synchronicities are only presented to us in that split second of a creative download, saying, "Look here!" It's where universal support and connection to our intuition are so crystal clear to us in the moment that it inspires us and kicks us into action without doubt, fear, or hesitation.

Intuitive Hits in the Moment

While synchronicities are noticed outside of ourselves, intuitive hits are an inner experience. Intuitive hits are gratitude and unconditional love magnified, and they are meant to arrive in the exact moment you receive them. No coincidences.

I believe that we all get intuitive hits, but they transmit differently depending on how we interpret them. It may be that we're at a traffic light and we just remembered that we need to call a friend because we were going to let them know something by today. That's an intuitive hit.

When intuitive hits are coming to us, giving clues about our next creation or significant leaps in soul growth, we are being urged to co-create something bigger than ourselves.

I have received a number of intuitive hits that have turned out to be ahead of their time. The ideas were downloaded to me, and I created something based on those downloads, but then it never went anywhere, until much later. It's like they had to incubate, get into the context of what they were supposed to be used for, and then activate.

When we start to notice these downloads of creative ideas coming to us in a flash, our spiritual gifts are expanded upon. The ideas come with so much inspiration that it's clear we have to act on them and express them in some form at that moment.

It's that point-of-no-return feeling again. That natural flow of what's around us at all times through nature, through our bodies, and through our inner voices and our hearts.

We're becoming part of the energetic message system of the planet. Downloads happen everywhere. But the downloads you receive via intuitive hits, however, are downloads that are meant just for you and only you.

When we are stressed, overworked, and worried, intuitive hits don't come through. Ideas of creation pass by like a highway of cars. When we are slowing down, tuning in to our natural energy, the transmission is clear. The spark of creation intuitively hits like a key in a lock, and off you go. Receiving it all in gratitude.

How can you slow down to receive intuitive hits?

Visualize Your Future Life Today

The practice of visualization and truly envisioning in the energy of your ideal dream life, as if that life were already here, is something that can help you make a quantum leap, without doing.

Energetically, visualization is like being in the here and now but leaping into the future. We're still preserving the "what is" or the here-and-now presence but we're also inviting the energy of being in our future. This is how we can put ourselves into our dream life without lifting a finger. No striving, no stress, no career path that requires climbing a ladder. We can just step into it for a moment!

Once I started to practice putting myself in the energy of my ideal dream life, it happened! Not necessarily right away, but as I write this, I'm truly amazed at the shift that has occurred for me.

As a result of this shift from pushing and wanting something different right away to allowing what I wanted to enter my reality in divine timing, I noticed my needs changed.

In my ideal dream life, I already had the financial security I needed. I already felt at ease since my day was full of flexibility, creativity, and time to myself. Therefore, my needs shifted and became related to living in balance and harmony within myself and with my environment.

The need to constantly judge myself and others shifted, and the need for acceptance and maintaining supportive thoughts to feel empowered became important. The need to push forward and get ahead to show others how capable I was and how well I could do something shifted into a strong need directly sourced from my soul to become a vessel of healing for others.

Just by diverting the focus on how dissatisfying my reality was at the time and instead immersing my energy in the vision of my ideal dream life, I created it by staying in the energy and the idea of what I wanted to manifest.

Shakti Gawain said in her book *Creative Visualization*, "The idea is like a blueprint; it creates an image of the form, which then magnetizes and guides the physical energy to flow into that form, and eventually manifests it on the physical plane."[56]

It sounds unbelievable, but once our soul recognizes that alignment with our ideal dream life, it falls into place. So if we play with an image of our ideal dream life and truly believe we can have it, we can start to experience it here and now. Let yourself experiment with no strings attached.

A simple way is to invite a different perspective of what you experience now. For example, instead of a firm holding on to a career as a safety net, connect with a limitless flow of inspiration from within to help direct your growth and expansion towards other potentially more suitable roles.

As you may have found already, the key is to play with the expansion so that the natural flow of energy can find you and inspire you from within. Then, all you have to do is trust it.

The fear of change often holds us back, as it did in my case, but if we believe that all is well, even during the most stressful times of our lives, the invitation is always there to imagine and play with a thought. And when we play with a thought in an expansive way, we play with natural expansive energy. Our reality is here and now, but when we invite our ideal dream life to be part of our reality, it happens in real time. Without effort or strife.

The most important thing is to not push with our will and force it. We can have it right away just by inviting the energy of our dream life here and now.

Manifestation Is Not Random

Manifestation is a result of you sending out positive energy to the Universe about what you welcome into your life with ease and effortless momentum. You have to mean it and you have to believe it.

---

[56] Shakti Gawain, *Creative Visualization: Use the Power of Your Imagination to Create What You Want in Your Life* (Novato: New World Library, 2010).

Like anything else, the Universe doesn't know what you want unless YOU know what you want and you ask for it. This also means that you turn over the power of making it happen to the Universe. How do you turn it over to the universe? Let go of the steps to get there.

Surrender.

Are you not seeing things happen in your life soon enough?

When you experience a standstill in your life is when you are pushing and controlling the most. You can't be in there redirecting and pushing it to come out a certain way or forcing it to come to life at the time you want things to happen. If you want momentum and want to know how to manifest whatever you want, it's time to welcome it! You may feel frustrated because you have a vision of what you want, but nothing happens…yet!

Many of us were taught that success in our modern society can only happen if you're "on" all the time. The word "proactive" has been the golden word for many years. Therefore, high-speed action all day long, thinking ahead, and reaching out is what we're taught. But there are other, easier ways to make changes or reach success. And it's very counterintuitive to what we're taught.

Want to learn how to manifest whatever you want?

Above all, for your life to change, you'll need to take responsibility for who you want to be in your life. It's only when we take full responsibility that things start to happen.

But you may say…

"I DID set some realistic goals this year, and STILL, nothing's happening!"

First, take a step back and consider setting an intention. Put your goals for the year on hold. Then, set an intention to welcome your wildest dreams into your life. This can feel scary. It can feel totally daunting to ask the universe to bring your dreams to life. It's totally understandable to feel like you're making a BIG leap. It's supposed to feel scary. That's when you know you're on the right track…

Lastly, to ease that scary feeling, to keep your courage, to ward off self-doubt and welcome support, keep believing in your intention every day of the year. Remind yourself of your intention every day. You will keep sending that positive energy, which is the essence of your intention, out into the universe, and POOF!

It's happening!!

Exercise:
Setting Intentions for
Manifestation

Before we get into the exercises for this chapter, I'd like to clear up a question that I often get asked: "What is the difference between an intention and a goal?"

* An intention is something you want to welcome into your life. You set the intention, and then you let it go. Release your intention to the Universe and trust it will happen. This way all possibilities are available for how this is going to come to realization for you.
* A goal is something you want to accomplish. A goal comes with a plan. Often a very detailed plan. Even though it makes us feel secure to have all the details planned out to get from A to B, with a goal, not all possibilities are available to you. By relying on the detail in your plan, you're limiting the solution.

This is important, as you may sense a significant difference in the energy frequency between an intention and a goal. Consider the energy in an intention of opportunity and potential versus the energy of a goal that is already defined.

Part I: Set Your Intention

In this exercise you'll set an intention for something you'd like to welcome into your life. Find a comfortable space where you can be undisturbed for at least 10 minutes.

"With ease I welcome _____ into my life."

1. Sit quietly with your closed eyes and pay attention to your inner feelings. Trust them. After you bring the vision of what you'd welcome into your life into your mind's eye, check to see how you feel inside.
   * If you feel happy and peaceful, you're on the right track.

   ✱ If you feel concerned or uncertain, it may not be the right time for that particular intention.

2. Ask yourself: Why do I want to welcome this into my life?
   Your intentions are truths for you. But beware, if your motive is based on anything else than your truth, it won't happen. So to be completely honest and use your intuition in this process of setting intentions. Trust the process.

3. Ask yourself: Who will this benefit?
   If your intention involves other people, you may want to only include your part of it. Setting intentions for others doesn't work. If your intention involves helping others, you can certainly include that this is part of your role.

4. Ask yourself: What within me is holding me back?
   Manifestation doesn't have any limits, so try not to be the limiting factor. Trust your ability to manifest, even if it sometimes feels like you're getting tested by life on the way there. Often, we limit ourselves by putting up external obstacles and reasons for not giving ourselves the opportunity to have what we want.

Part II: Making a Decision with Gratitude

With this three-step exercise you'll increase the feeling of gratitude and trust in yourself and your ability to make decisions by using your intuition and these guiding steps:

1. Feel gratitude for how you got to this point.
   All of us have gone through both good and bad situations and experiences in our lives. Often, we're not so grateful for the bad times, the hardships we've experienced. It could be getting laid off at work, losing a loved one, or living in a relationship with someone that hurt you.
   You may think, *It's not ever going to be possible to feel grateful for all the bad things that have happened!* I'd challenge you to look more closely at those situations that you're resisting feeling gratitude for the most.
   Pick one or two of the most challenging situations/experiences you've had and ask yourself: "In hindsight, what did I learn

from that experience?" What was life trying to tell you? Write down what comes up. No edits, just what you learned and any life lessons you experienced as a result of that challenging situation.

Now you're ready to go to the next step.

2. Feel gratitude for You today.

    Today is your real life. The past is in the past, even if it feels like yesterday. That's why it's so important to make decisions based on today and not the past. If you have a big decision to make today, let's base it on today.

    Below is a simple exercise to help awaken the energy of gratitude.

    * Take out a piece of paper and a pen. Writing it down is making it real.
    * Write down 10 people you are grateful for having in your life right now.
    * Write down a sentence about each person and why you are grateful for them.
    * Look at the sentences.
    * The sentences that you wrote down are exactly what you are grateful for about YOURSELF today.
    * Understandably, this may not make sense to you, but our relationships are a reflection of ourselves. Everything you're grateful for in others you have in you as well.

    But how is this related to decision making? Your decisions are under the direction of how you feel about yourself. Self-love is key to manifestation.

    For example, if you're not trusting yourself and your ability to make decisions, the likelihood of making the right decision for you is limited.

3. Make a tuned-in decision based on your truth.

    By increasing your ability to feel gratitude and love for both yourself and your life, you are accessing your truth. In addition, you're going to arrive at your truth using your intuition. Your intuition is flowing freely in a centered state.

    You can access your intuition in two to three minutes. You don't have to meditate that long to get tuned in.

Accessing your decision through your intuition can be as easy as these simple steps below:

* Sit down somewhere comfortable with your feet on the ground.
* Close your eyes and take a deep breath in through your nose.
* Notice all the thoughts that are swirling around inside your head.
* Take in another deep inhale through your nose, hold it for two seconds, and then exhale all of that through your mouth.
* Notice how you feel and bring the image of your situation of where you need to decide into your mind.
* Keep your eyes closed and ask your inner self: "What's the right decision?"
* Listen to the answer. Write it down right away, no edits. It may not make sense right away, but it's the answer. Trust it!
* If you feel torn or don't like what you wrote down, you likely tried to make it into an answer; you tried too hard. Your truth is always going to make you feel good.
* Surrender and repeat.

18
Shift 7: From Individual to Multidimensional

> *"Keep your eyes on the stars and*
> *your feet on the ground."*
> — Theodore Roosevelt

I wake up with the images still lingering from the night's dream. I lie completely still with my eyes closed, adjusting to the newness of a new day. I sense the sun rising as a band of light comes through my curtain. It feels like it's going to be yet another awesome day. The sun's beams energize me; they give me hope.

I feel a sense of anticipation for the new day. I'm feeling curious and open to creating. *What is today going to be like? What messages will I receive? What synchronicities will I experience today? How will I deepen my connection to life?*

As I lay there, still in bed, not yet opening my eyes, I feel my energy awaken. I'm returning from spending time at some place far away and back into my body and awareness.

I write down any thoughts or images from my dreams. I have noticed that what I write down as I catch fragments of my dreams is pure creativity, unbound and free from mental interpretation, sourced directly from my higher true self as it remains in union with the Universe for just a bit longer.

For a moment, I feel completely one with all that exists. As soon as I open my eyes, my mind is thinking, *Aaah I can't wait for the coffee!* It's one of the things that kicks me in gear in the morning. I even have

WISDOM BEYOND WHAT YOU KNOW

a small coffee maker in my bedroom, and just by thinking about that cup of coffee I'm about to enjoy, I come back to this reality and wake up completely! I make my coffee and I get ready for meditation.

Nowadays, I love my morning time. I don't get out of my bedroom until late morning, sometimes later. It's my sacred time, meditating in communion with my spirit guides and the Universe to exchange a conversation, receiving guidance, healing, and messages.

I maintain a careful journal where I record the daily messages that I receive. Following meditation most days, I also spend time connecting with my body and listening to what it's telling me through yoga or energy work and breathwork.

This sets the stage for how I maintain my sense of connectedness through each day. In my experience, a daily practice is the foundation for inner work to integrate and help us continue on our soul path. My true self is trying to make me realize that I need to know I can come back to feeling calm and centered every day, not just when I think I need it. I need something that can help me return to my center every day. I don't want to feel my day to be like a hit and miss anymore. I want harmony and balance. Every day.

My daily practice is a way for my heart and my inner voice to stay intertwined for yet another day.

My time in communion with the Universe, my inner voice, and my true self is sacred. I won't start my day without it. It's a profound change in my day to day that has had the greatest impact on my life so far.

Harmonizing with the Universe

I believe that multidimensional living is when we expand ourselves to relate to and live in harmony and balance not only with ourselves and what is around us but also with that which is unseen.

When we allow ourselves to open up to a multidimensional perspective, we embrace living in daily communion with what is truth, consciousness, and creativity.

A single-dimensional perspective lends itself to a linear, logic- and mind-driven existence, where we experience high levels of distraction, stress, and unbalance. It's an individualistic feeling of separation from each other, striving to do as many things as possible at the same time. Multidimensional living, on the other hand, is a life of co-creation, joy, love, harmony, balance, and unity.

I believe that multidimensional living is available to us today, and we are only a decision away. We can decide between our current structured existence and multidimensional living once we realize that we're only living through a single dimension right now, which is based on what we can see and touch; living this way and, in addition, subscribing to a perspective of individuality places limitations on us.

As we stand on the verge of significant opportunities for inner transformation and expansion as a collective, we are faced with a renewed commitment to our truth. A commitment to get out of the comfort zone and to step into multidimensional living to receive a different result, where we apply different values, beliefs, and actions to create a life beyond what our ego minds know now.

Multidimensional living is a transformation into the essence of "we and us" instead of "me and them." It is a new sense of balance in the collective of harmony and peace for all.

Imagine...

* a life where we fully get to know and express our innate talents and gifts in unlimited combinations, rather than placing ourselves on a predetermined, socially accepted career path.
* a life where we are valued and contribute based on our talents and gifts.
* a life where demonstration of self-awareness and self-love is a prerequisite for any relationship.
* a life where we naturally come together to create life-changing healing and solutions for all rather than being served an answer by a few.

The list goes on...

But before all of that, there is one invitation that is extended to each one of us—to develop a spiritual practice where we integrate our experience consistently. I believe everyone can benefit from a spiritual practice, especially if we want to live a multidimensional life.

A spiritual practice involves creating a daily energetic container where we intend to get to know ourselves at the level of the true self so that we can intentionally make the shift from being driven by the mind to living from the heart and intuition. It is within our spiritual practice our journey of expansion toward a multidimensional life begins.

One morning, I was working with a client who felt so completely stuck. My client sat down in front of her computer to start our session. I could see that she was making a face as her body hit the chair. Her body was feeling stiff and achy, especially in the hip area. She had wrestled with overwhelm for an extended period of time, trying to build a business on the side while working overtime at her regular job.

"I feel so frustrated," she said. "I am working so hard but I don't feel I make any progress," she let the words out with a sigh.

Frustrated, she continued, "The only thing I can see is the mountain of work, and I feel scattered due to many different priorities. I don't know how I'm going to make progress. Next week is going to be a nightmare!" Her eyes expanded with hopelessness and sadness at the same time, then she looked down.

The feeling of treading water, putting so much effort in but not making progress, had made her start to doubt that she had made the right move by starting that side business.

"Thank you for sharing how you feel. With so much to do it's no wonder that you can see only the mountain of work," I said softly.

Then I continued, "Do you remember when you first started to dream about shifting into full-time entrepreneurship? Would you like to visit that dream again?"

"Yes, YES! I can't remember when I thought of that last. Must have been months and months ago..." she said with hidden hesitation in her voice.

"Let's go there right now." With a deep breath we started the meditation. I guided her to tap into the feeling of what she wanted to create meant to her and helped her to connect with what her soul truly needed at this time.

When I guided her true self to tell her what she needed, she said, "I see a beach."

"What else do you see?" I asked with curiosity.

"I look out over the sea and I sit down. I just want to sit down and rest," she said.

As I gently guided her to tap into her subconscious, decoding the images symbolizing her deepest desires, I could see her body relax, and as she went deeper into the imagery and feelings, her face muscles relaxed, changing her facial expression.

Her body knew.

After spending another few minutes exploring, I gently guided her out of the meditation and back to reality.

Immediately, she blurted out, "I have been focusing on what I don't want! What if I start focusing on what I WANT, instead of putting all my energy towards being frustrated not getting there?" After a few moments, she said, "Thank you. I feel so much better," now with a calm voice and smiling without hesitation.

Just connecting back to her heart's creative flowing energy for a few minutes took her right to the energy of her deepest desires instead of maintaining the mind's chaotic, one-sided automatic transfer belt of work-harder messages.

Naturally, the meditation had provided her with an opening to connect with her heart, and her perception of her situation changed.

A perception shift can take a second, a lifetime, or may never happen at all. But when it happens, it's an experience within you, and the body is totally on board.

As Maggie Lyon in *Experience Life* said, "Ultimately, we must summon the courage to make room for spiritual practice, and the experiment that it is, as instigator at any given time of peace, elation, chill out, aha, tears, or evocative reflection. We must be willing to face whatever arises within this uncanny vehicle and to touch the sacred in ourselves every precious day."[57]

When you have a shift in perception, a release happens in the body energetically as well as physically. All of a sudden, you may feel physical symptoms, such as sudden coughing or a leg moving into a cramp without warning. The energetic release in the body of experiencing that cough or cramp immediately brings discomfort but also a sensation of connection, calm, and grounding, and a natural solution to the resistance you may experience in the moment.

Your true self and your body know what is best for you.

---

[57] Maggie Lyon, "The Benefits of Spiritual Practice," Experience Life, Last accessed Nov 2, 2021, https://experiencelife.lifetime.life/article/the-benefits-of-spiritual-practice/.

On Your Way to Self-Mastery

With a regular spiritual practice you give yourself the chance to slow down enough to contemplate, identify, and evaluate your own patterns and change your perspective.

One of the biggest reasons for not seeing what's possible for us is that we focus on the *effort* that we have to put in, and we don't envision what a spiritual practice can *make possible*. This perception shift from focusing on effort as opposed to expanding a vision is important in the shift to multidimensional living. With a daily practice, we can tap into this vast knowledge of the body and true self daily.

Perception shifts like the one for my client previously described may support to establish positive experiences of daily life and allow your future dreams to start to manifest. For example, if your true self says yes, but your ego says it's going to be too much effort, consider a perception shift where you let go of the self-doubt and allow yourself to focus on what is possible for you rather than the daily effort you put in.

When we're not prioritizing ourselves and our needs, it often comes with a lack of belief in ourselves or lack of boundaries with others. The self-doubt created is keeping us away from the unique universal support that is there for us to tap into.

When we are not devoting time daily to tend to our own deep soul needs through grounding self-care practices, we don't connect to self-love in the heart and we're not satisfying our need for self-love. As previously discussed, self-love opens our energy up to receive cosmic support and facilitates manifestation.

The container of inner peace and calm that we create daily through a spiritual practice is THAT valuable. It's that soul nourishing to us that it cannot be knocked off the throne of importance.

Imagine a practice that does not feel like a practice in the traditional sense. It's simply a life-changing way of showing up every day that can be just as transformational as the way we change as we grow up and change perspectives from being a child or teen to becoming an adult. It's a different way to relate.

Having a spiritual, day-to-day practice is about self-mastery, feeding ourselves self-love, and strengthening our relationship to our heart energy and our connection to the Universe.

I like this definition of self-mastery: "Self-mastery is being in control of the internal thought processes that guide your emotions, habits, and behaviors. It's the ability to respond rather than react."[58]

On that same note, self-love can only be given by ourselves to ourselves, and that is what makes us grow our connection to our hearts. When we practice this, we can stand in our power, and we will no longer need validation from someone else or something on the outside.

As our spiritual practice takes root within, the desire to share our heart energy with others grows. The overflow of calm grounding and inner peace radiates out naturally.

The continued, daily connection with our inner voice and the ability to experience new heights of expansion within the direction of our soul's path gets more and more important as time goes on. We focus less and less on what we can get from others to further our goals.

A spiritual practice can help us out of stuck feelings or stagnant situations as they come up on a daily basis. A daily practice can help us stay grounded in our experience of life, and it can teach us to sit down and feel joy for life just as it is.

Starting and returning to a spiritual practice every day becomes easier once we experience the transformational impact it has on our entire well-being. For me, without the daily connection with myself, I'm right back to where I once was—scattered, closed up, and feeling like I'm not enough. There is no doubt in my mind about what a daily spiritual practice provides for me.

In my experience, a spiritual practice is a gateway to a self-sufficient loop of self-love, which overturns that need to always receive validation from outside of us and transforms it into unconditional giving and being from within.

However, importantly, the spiritual practice is not something that can be inherited or copied as a quick fix. A practice that provides transformational power requires commitment, but when we do undertake this journey, we grow our souls and mature from a needy child to an adult expressing self-mastery.

---

[58] "Success Starts with Self-Mastery: 7 Effective Strategies," Skip Richard, Last accessed Nov 2, 2021, https://www.skipprichard.com/success-starts-with-self-mastery-7-effective-strategies/.

Only we know within ourselves what self-mastery means for us individually. And when a spiritual practice is established, we have a consistent way to explore and embody that self-mastery.

An Endless Journey

The work is done every day. Every minute of life. Even if we're not thinking, we're doing it. I used to think there was an end goal to what I wanted to accomplish. Because we are taking these actions every day, we think the destination is around the corner. But it isn't. It's endless.

I wonder if the mind wants us to spend our time thinking we're almost done; just another day, and we'll be done. Sometimes it feels like if we only do this, or learn this, or reach for more of that, we're going to make it, and we'll be OK for the rest of our lives. That's not true. There will always be a new experience that we're ready for, another corner to turn.

So why don't we just relax within all the action and movement around and within us? Why don't we just lie down on the raft, look up at the sky, and let ourselves be rocked from side to side as we go down the river of experiences in life, instead of trying to get to shore because we think that's going to help us get to where we need to go.

There is a paradigm shift here when it comes to appreciating the soft, gentle rocking of life that knows how to bring us forward. This shift does not reveal itself when our raft is too cluttered with rocks that weigh us down; it only seems to be present once we ensure our raft is free flowing consistently through life's movement with lightness of heart.

That's why it's key to believe that it's possible to lie there on the raft with your gaze on the stars until the end of time. So how do we get to that space within, where we can float indefinitely with life as if we were carried by a lazy river?

In my experience, the key is to keep maintaining the flow of that comforting pace of the lazy river every day, with me in it.

A deepened awareness and practice with nature helped me to welcome more balance, peace, trust, and contentment as a means to effortless manifestation and helped me to shift out of the exhausting energy of multitasking and push to a goal.

Our energy body is closely connected to our surrounding energy environment. We can ground ourselves by visualizing our connection

SHIFT 7: FROM INDIVIDUAL TO MULTIDIMENSIONAL

with the energy of the Earth (which is often done at the beginning of meditation), but it's not the same as actually bringing our energy body to physically connecting and grounding with the Earth itself. So, for example, if you're not spending that much time outside looking up to the sun, touching a tree, or walking on the surface of the Earth, the energy body doesn't get the re-charge and alignment with the Earth that it needs.

Through our heart energy, our ability to blend with the Earth and the Universal energy of love comes naturally. The reason the mind is not driven by love is because the mind is driven by duality. The duality of right and wrong, good and bad, and me and them. But as soon as we come in contact with our heart energy of love, we feel the connection to the greater power available to us that is connected to the whole where there is no duality, only oneness, and unity.

A Broadened Perspective

Multidimensional living means that we have shifted our perspective about ourselves and what we are. When we relate through living from the heart and intuition, we believe that we can remember the wisdom that our soul holds inside.

This could, for example, be to view our life as much greater than this lifetime; our life becomes equal to our soul's journey through the past and into future lifetimes. We might view our soul and its lessons as far greater than what we currently believe about ourselves.

This also comes with the curiosity to learn more about our past lives and lessons and also how we can extend into utilizing our gifts and talents in future lives. The carrier and director of this is our soul, our true self. In this case, staying aligned with our true self becomes so much more important.

One way of relating to our soul's journey is through the Akashic Records, which is defined as "a record of each soul's journey through the infinite."[59] Our individual record could be described as the soul presence of our true self through our soul's journey of past, present, and future that we constantly have access to. As we expand and relate

---

[59] "Akashic Records 101: Can We Access Our Akashic Records?," Gaia, Last accessed Nov 2, 2021, https://www.gaia.com/article/akashic-records-101-can-we-access-our-akashic-records.

beyond the physical, we would also consider our Akashic record as a source of information as we live our life.

Equally, the interest in the role of the Earth and Universe expands, and we may become much more concerned with the ecosystem of the Earth and planetary movements to help us stay aligned with our true self and consciousness. We may live from the perspective of energy and choose to engage in work and activities that hold as high of a frequency as possible; therefore, we may begin to believe that alchemy and anything is possible.

Through inner exploration and practice, we may naturally expand our intuitive abilities, such as telepathy and channeling, where messages may take on a more synchronistic and multisensory nature.

All of this is supported by a daily spiritual practice and an energy of calm, creativity, love, and compassion.

This is the energy that many of you are connecting with already! As the energy travels in its natural way through you, blending with the energy of the Earth, the Universe, and your heart, you are presented with the opportunity to support others to get to know their true selves so that we all can align with ease and flow and feel balance emotionally, spiritually, mentally, and physically.

Through the spiritual day-to-day you practice a deepened commitment to yourself not just at the task level but to your soul. Ultimately, it's a practice of surrender, receiving, and giving love to yourself and others in a way that you may not have experienced before.

Exercise:
A Multidimensional Experience

Throughout this book we've explored what I hope will be life-changing shifts for you. In this last exercise, we connect to some of the key aspects of multidimensional living through grounding, connecting with your talents and gifts, how you want to feel, and possibility.

The platform for doing all of that is a daily spiritual practice and eventually, the ability to take action, share, and connect with your community.

Part I: Grounding

The more time we spend getting to know our unique connection with the Earth for ourselves, the more we'll recognize when we are aligned with the natural flow that nature offers us, and we'll also notice when we're not grounded and aligned with it.

One way of checking with your own grounding is to take 10 minutes to sit still, close your eyes and connect to the Earth and the Universe, feeling the enveloping, powerful creative energy from the Earth and the light energy from the Universe.

Part II: Connect with Your Talents and Gifts

Everyone has an innate talent for something. To reconnect with your talents, go back to what you used to love to do as a child, the things that you do naturally, the things that light you up.

It's natural to forget, but spend some time going back to those moments when you truly felt alive. That's the starting point to explore.

Part III: Connect with How You Want to Feel

Many of us live our lives complaining and feeling frustrated, worried, and stressed because that's how most people chose to approach their day, even if it feels like resistance.

* Connecting with your desired feelings is about turning this automatic mindset of complaining on its head.
* Go deep into what feelings you'd like to feel every day of your life — and not just how you want to feel when you come home in the evening after work. Connect with your desired feelings for EVERY area in your life.
* Your life is linked together; so are your feelings.

Part IV: Connect with Possibility

By connecting with possibility I mean connecting with the DREAM of your WILDEST dreams. Allow yourself to dream BIG!

* If you feel like you don't have any big dreams, that's not true!
* Watch out for your inner dialogue. Notice what that voice is telling you. Your inner critic is holding you back! You can instantly give your inner critic a new job.
* The truth is that if you don't feel your dreams are big enough, think about the last time you failed. What was the worst thing that happened?
* If you don't believe in your dream with conviction, it's not going to happen.
* We all want to feel protected, that's natural, but are you playing it safe with what you know is not going to make you happy? How are you going to show up differently? This step is huge!

If your dream still feels quite unreachable, how do you start putting all of this into action?

Break your dream down into something you feel is doable every day — maybe even just a small part of your day to start with.

Part V: Create a Spiritual Practice

A multidimensional life includes a spiritual practice. Deepen your existing practice or create one. One of the most powerful ways to make a change that'll last is by starting a new daily morning practice that you LOVE! How do you feel when you wake up in the morning? Do you live your dream? Below are a few suggestions to get you started.

* If you start your day in a rush, with a to-do list that's already full, thinking about what needs to be done at work and home, you likely feel overwhelmed and stressed.
* If you start your day by connecting with yourself, journaling your thoughts out on a page without edits, in gratitude, setting an intention for the day to come, you'll start your day feeling calm and connected.
* Ask your true self and your guides for answers and notice down what comes through.

When you start a new morning routine and get curious about yourself and your life in a different way, it's an opportunity to start a new practice that can stay with you for a lifetime.

When you apply the three steps above and change your mornings, you'll cultivate a mindset shift from your rush-go-go external focus to invite your quiet, whispering true self. What happens is that you'll replace the focus on what needs to be done today with an internal focus where you honor how you want to feel and why.

This shift can be life changing. Commit today. Practice in appreciation and acceptance of yourself.

Part VI: Take Action

Ask yourself: What's the one little thing that's going to make the difference for me right now?

This is the question that you can ask yourself anytime you feel you're off-the-charts busy. You need realistic shifts that make a difference instantly, not the sweeping goals of "One day I'll..." If you're going to live a life in well-being, it starts in this moment. (Try it out! Ask yourself right now: "What is that one little thing that's going to make the difference for me right now?")

Maybe it's that you're reaching for your headphones and finally doing that three-minute meditation, or you're deciding that tomorrow you'll set your alarm for 10 minutes earlier and start a completely new morning routine.

Part VII: Connect to Community

If you want to live a multidimensional life and maintain that for a long time, you'll need to take the focus off yourself and onto how you can share your talents and gifts to help, influence, or teach others.

When you're creating space for yourself, you're pushing stress and busyness away by taking your attention off yourself. Use your talents to stay true to who you are, go for it, own your awesomeness, and share it with the world!!!

CONCLUSION

> *"You'll never find peace until you listen to your heart."*
> — George Michael

After that surprising phone call a few years ago, I discovered that I could feel better. The most amazing part is that the situation catapulted me into a change beyond what I knew at the time, and I set out on an inner journey that led me to change my life and take it in a completely new direction.

I realized that there is more to this human experience than rushing around and getting things done.

Looking back, there's profound gratitude for what happened to me, and the reward is the trust I'm experiencing now in myself and life at a completely different level than ever before. I got the firsthand experience that there is beauty in absolutely everything. Including myself. Beauty is there and happening whether we notice it or not.

I know that if I had gone on to another cycle of the same patterns, I wouldn't have yet been able to experience life with the vivid colors and self-love that I do now.

There is a depth of love that we have access to in our daily lives, but we rarely take the time to slow down and bathe in it in our modern world. It's a love that is worth all the suffering we have to go through on our way to greater wisdom. Acquiring this wisdom is what we came here to experience. We came here to learn the life lessons we want to learn and to gain that perspective. When we live from the heart, those soul life lessons don't feel like work anymore; they are love. Self-love.

In this book, we've covered examples of some of the most common patterns of mind-driven living and we've explored some of the key aspects of heart-centered living. Most importantly, we've learned about the seven shifts that are available to us right now and are lovingly directing us towards an expanded consciousness beyond the physical experience and towards unity consciousness.

The inner journey of awakening to our own wisdom can be described as our path to increase our capacity to love ourselves and others. If we can commit and take responsibility for our own well-being and true inner needs at the individual level, we can continue our quest to know our innate talents and gifts so that we can contribute and share them with others and the world for the benefit of all.

There is a quest to know more about and connect with the unseen and the Universe as a whole; to not only integrate and utilize natural laws in our daily life but also live and embody our best life here in harmony with the Earth.

Bill Bowerman, co-founder of Nike, said, "Everything you need is inside." At this time, many are gaining the insight that we have all we need within us to live a happy life and that it has been within us all along. That we don't need to seek the answer outside of us anymore. This profound insight turns the direction of our energy from external to internal.

With this focus we can expand our daily perspective to include the influence of energy and the unseen support we have available to us in the forms of spirit guides and synchronicities to become as mainstream as the internet is today.

Like Nicola Tesla once suggested, we have the opportunity to merge our mind-driven science with heart-centered spirituality and co-create with the Universe like never before. I believe the way we will use our expanded abilities and how we relate to the vast wisdom that is in the unseen will be a breakthrough for humanity.

To align with the natural laws of the Universe and flow with them in its highest frequency may activate developments and abilities beyond our current human senses, but it starts with tapping into the heart and intuition and letting go of outdated mind-driven beliefs about ourselves and what is possible.

It starts with breaking through the fear and merging with the Earth and the Universe to start sharing and giving back through a purpose that is larger than ourselves.

What happens next?

The content of this book can be broken down into the following questions that you are encouraged to find the answers to within yourself over time. This is best done supported by a daily spiritual practice. The questions are designed to give you focus as you continue on your path.

1. Who are you?
2. What are your talents and gifts?
3. What do you want?
4. What makes you happy?
5. How has your past influenced you?
6. How can you contribute to a sustainable planet?
7. What are your life lessons?
8. How can you express your inner truth?
9. What are you afraid of?
1. How can you receive?
2. How does your energy work?
1. How do you want to feel?
2. What are your energetic boundaries?
3. How can you be a role model for others to make a shift for themselves?

The key for you to experience transformation fully is to implement what you've learned about yourself in this book over time.

It's an inside journey, first and foremost, but it's also a collective journey. The individual journey is the work, but having a group of likeminded people is important, too. The journey is yours. The support and shared experience are in the collective.

When you express your gifts and talents with passion, based in self-love and motivation from within, you share and contribute authentically to your community and the world as a whole.

There's going to be a greater need for us all to come together to provide support for each other to maintain our inner energy flow and grounding as we expand our connection to our true self and the Universe as we proceed further into this decade and beyond.

After you finish this book, you are invited to continue this journey through the seven shifts. You are encouraged to take your time integrating your experience of heart-centered living by starting and maintaining a consistent spiritual practice (if you don't already have one) as a foundation for lifelong spiritual growth. You can find more information on how to continue what you started on https://wisdombeyondbook.com.

The opportunity you have is to begin co-creating together in harmony and balance with the Earth and the Universe.

It's wisdom beyond what you know. Trust.

ACKNOWLEDGMENTS

I would like to thank my loving family, my husband, Jim, and our daughters, Svea, Elsa, and Alma, for making it possible for me to write this book. Thank you to my mom, Gunnel, my dad, Rolf, and my sister, Caroline, for being mirrors of inspiration, love, and learning throughout my life.

Thank you to my book team. Kristen, thank you for always being steps ahead in the book process and for your guidance through many key decisions to make this book the best possible. Maira, your sense of what works out there is spot on and has been invaluable in bringing this book to the world. Zora, thank you for your professional editing expertise and efficiency from the first draft to book and beyond.

To my many clients, there was only room for snapshots of a few client stories in this book, but you all know who you are. Through working with each one of you, your soul transformations are captured within my heart forever.

To all my friends, especially my dear yogi friends, Shagufta, Carin, and Laura, for totally getting the stick figures I drew on my arm so I could remember my first yoga sequence. We all are better humans thanks to our journey together.

Thank you to all my iPEC coach peers. I witnessed my own transformation through being coached by many of you. The breakthrough of believing wholeheartedly within my core that I could shift from a predictable, stable, high-paying career to take a risk and become a first-time business owner changed my life, thanks to the power of the coaching process.

To Karissa Eve and Bindy, amazing spiritual teachers from whom I've learned so much about Spirit and energy, thank you for helping me open up to my own gifts.

To Sarah, for being an inspiration and role model to me. Ever since we met a few years ago, when your first book was published, I knew I wanted to write a book myself. Thank you to the women of Tribe Inside for your heart and support through a time we all needed it the most.

To my friend and coach Alicia, who came into my world right on time to hold space for me as I was writing this book, you are a gem.

I am eternally grateful to my Spirit guides who are always near and have been communicating with us (through me and this book) what we need to understand at this time in our lives to shift to heart-centered living.

To my readers:

You are a divine soul.
You now have the wisdom it takes to live a full life here on Earth.
Knowing what's right and wrong for you.
Being sovereign is the start from where you grow and flourish for real.
Your gifts are laid out for you to receive and pick up along the way.
The unique combination of your energy.
As independent as a star.
As needed as a part of the ecosystem.
The experience of your life is here and now.
Not before, not later.
It's a special day.
It's today.

ABOUT THE AUTHOR

Ulrika Sullivan is an intuitive spiritual life coach (CPC, ELI-MP), yoga instructor (RYT-200), and energy healer (Usui Reiki II).

After leaving a multitasking corporate career, stressed out and disconnected from herself, Ulrika realized she didn't know who she truly was. This catalyzed a complete inner shift and awakening, leading her to what she calls her "point of no return" and a new direction. Now she knows *exactly* what she is here to do and share with the world.

Ever since, Ulrika has been successfully helping others to connect with their own intuition, find their calm, and reconnect with their true self and self-love to live with more ease and flow. With positive, empowering encouragement, she provides a consistent space for daily spiritual practice alongside powerful private coaching and healing sessions.

For more inspiration, visit her website ulrikasullivan.com and check out her podcast, *New Light Living – See Your Life in a New Light.*

Instagram @ulrikasullivan

YouTube Ulrika Sullivan - Intuitive Spiritual Life Coach

Facebook @ulrikasullivancoach

LinkedIn @usullivan

Pinterest @ulrikasullivan

Twitter @SullivanUlrika

Join the *Beyond the Mind* membership to stay centered
and step into multidimensional living every day!

Learn more here:
ulrikasullivan.com/beyondthemind

BIBLIOGRAPHY

"7 Tips to Strengthen Your Intuition and Take Soul-Inspired Action."
Jack Canfield. Last accessed Nov 2, 2021. https://www.jackcanfield.
com/blog/cultivating-intuition/.

Ackerman, Courtney E. "What is Self-Compassion and What is Self-
Love?." Positive Psychology. Last accessed Nov 2, 2021. https://
positivepsychology.com/self-compassion-self-love/.

Allen A.B. and Leary M.R. Self-Compassion, Stress, and Coping.
Social and Personality Psychology Compass 4, no.2 (2010):107-118.
doi:10.1111/j.1751-9004.2009.00246.x.

"Akashic Records 101: Can We Access Our Akashic Records?" Gaia.
Last accessed Nov 2, 2021 https://www.gaia.com/article/akashic-
records-101-can-we-access-our-akashic-records.

Astrodienst. Last accessed Nov 2, 2021. https://astro.com.

Athar, Kiran. "11 Signs of a Spiritual Awakening Ending Your
Relationship." HackSpirit. Last accessed Nov 2, 2021. https://
hackspirit.com/spiritual-awakenings-ending-your-relationship/.

"Awareness of Self." Earl E. Bakken Center for Spirituality & Healing,
University of Minnesota. Last accessed Nov 2, 2021. https://www.csh.
umn.edu/education/focus-areas/whole-systems-healing/leadership/
awareness-self.

Alton, Liz. "The Evolution From Work-Life Balance to Work-Life
Integration." ADP. Last accessed Nov 2, 2021. https://www.adp.com/
spark/articles/2018/10/the-evolution-from-work-life-balance-to-work-
life-integration.aspx.

Bardwick, Judith M. *Danger in the Comfort Zone: From Boardroom to
Mailroom; How to Break the Entitlement Habit That's Killing American
Business* (New York: American Management Association, 1995).

Brown, Brené. "Dare to Lead Hub; Workbook, Glossary, and Art Pics." Last accessed Nov 2, 2021. https://daretolead.brenebrown.com/workbook-art-pics-glossary/.

Capacchione, Lucia. *Recovery of Your Inner Child* (New York: Simon & Schuster, 1991).

Cahn, Lauren. "You're Spending Too Much Time Inside If This Happens to Your Body." Health Digest. Last accessed Nov 2, 2021. https://www.healthdigest.com/281265/youre-spending-too-much-time-inside-if-this-happens-to-your-body/.

Chopra, Deepak and Kafatos, Menas. *You Are The Universe: Discovering Your Cosmic Self and Why It Matters* (New York City: Harmony, 2017).

COBUILD Advanced English Dictionary. HarperCollins Publishers. Last accessed Nov 2, 2021. https://www.collinsdictionary.com/us/dictionary/english/aura.

Davis, Tchiki. "What Is Manifestation? Science-Based Ways to Manifest." Psychology Today. Last accessed Nov 2, 2021. https://www.psychologytoday.com/ca/blog/click-here-happiness/202009/what-is-manifestation-science-based-ways-manifest.

Dunion, Paul. "Unity Consciousness." Huffpost. Last accessed Nov 2, 2021. https://www.huffpost.com/entry/unity-consciousness_b_8244982.

Eden, Donna and Feinstein, David. *Energy Medicine: Balancing Your Body's Energies for Optimal Health, Joy, and Vitality* (Los Angeles: Jeremy P. Tarcher, 2008).

Estrada, Jessica. "No, It's Not Just a Coincidence—Here's How to Spot and Decode Spiritual Synchronicities." Well+Good. Last accessed Nov 2, 2021. https://www.wellandgood.com/what-does-synchronicity-mean-spiritually/.

Ferrer, Jorge N. "What Does It Mean to Live A Fully Embodied Life?." *International Journal of Transpersonal Studies* 27 (2008): pp 1-11.

Fox, Mia. "The Power of Gratitude for Manifesting." Self Made Ladies. Last accessed Nov 2, 2021. https://selfmadeladies.com/power-gratitude-manifesting/.

Friedman, Stewart D. *Total Leadership: Be a Better Leader Have a Richer Life*. Boston: Harvard Business Review Press, 2008.

Fujita, Kara Jovic. "Tapping into the Mind–Body Connection." Wanderlust. Last accessed Nov 2, 2021. https://wanderlust.com/journal/tapping-the-bodys-inherent-wisdom/.

Gawain, Shakti. *Creative Visualization: Use the Power of Your Imagination to Create What You Want in Your Life*. Novato: New World Library, 2010.

Harvard Medical School. "Yoga Benefits Beyond the Mat." Harvard Health Publishing. https://www.health.harvard.edu/staying-healthy/yoga-benefits-beyond-the-mat.

Hawkins, David R. "Map of Consciousness®." Veritas Publishing. https://veritaspub.com/product/map-of-consciousness-dr-david-hawkins/.

Helliwell, John F. et al. "World Happiness Report 2021." Last accessed Nov 2, 2021. https://worldhappiness.report/.

Hull, Megan. "Work Addiction Statistics." The Recovery Village. Last accessed Nov 2, 2021. https://www.therecoveryvillage.com/process-addiction/work-addiction/work-addiction-statistics/.

Julia, Fp. "Radiant Human." Bldg25. Last accessed Nov 2, 2021. https://blog.freepeople.com/2016/03/radiant-human/.

Jones, Heather. "What Is Codependency?." Verywellhealth. Last accessed Nov 2, 2021. https://www.verywellhealth.com/codependency-5093171.

Jovian Archive. Last accessed Nov 2, 2021. https://jovianarchive.com/.

Lancer, Darlene. "Meeting Your Needs Is the Key to Happiness." PsychCentral. Last accessed Nov 2, 2021. https://psychcentral.com/lib/meeting-your-needs-is-the-key-to-happiness#1.

Legg, Timothy J. "Codependency: How Emotional Neglect Turns Us into People-Pleasers." Healthline. Last accessed Nov 2, 2021. https://www.healthline.com/health/mental-health/codependency-and-attachment-trauma.

Lyon, Maggie. "The Benefits of Spiritual Practice." Experience Life. Last accessed Nov 2, 2021. https://experiencelife.lifetime.life/article/the-benefits-of-spiritual-practice/.

Martin, Sharon. "How I Transformed my Self-Criticism into Self-Love." PsychCentral. Last accessed Nov 2, 2021. https://psychcentral.com/blog/imperfect/2020/02/how-i-transformed-my-self-criticism-into-self-love#Transform-self-criticism-into-self-acceptance.

Merriam-Webster.com Dictionary. Merriam-Webster. Last accessed Nov 2, 2021. https://www.merriam-webster.com/dictionary/people%20pleaser.

Miller, GE. "70% of Americans want to be Self-Employed. What is Stopping you?." 20SomethingFinance. Last accessed Nov 2, 2021. https://20somethingfinance.com/self-employment-poll/.

Mental Health America. "Co-Dependency". Last accessed Nov 2, 2021. https://www.mhanational.org/co-dependency.

Mertins, Brian. "Beginner's Guide to Developing Intuition with Rewilding." Nature Mentoring. Last accessed Nov 2, 2021. https://nature-mentor.com/intuition-and-rewilding/.

Nordstrom-Loeb, Barbara. "Embodiment - How to get it and why it is important." Earl E. Bakken Center for Spirituality & Healing; University of Minnesota. Last accessed Nov 2, 2021. https://www.csh.umn.edu/news-events/blog/thoughts-about-embodiment-how-get-it-and-why-it-important.

Page, Oliver. "How to Leave Your Comfort Zone and Enter Your 'Growth Zone'." Positive Psychology. Last accessed Nov 2, 2021. https://positivepsychology.com/comfort-zone/.

Parker, Ceri. "It's Official: Women Work Nearly an Hour Longer Than Men Every Day." World Economic Forum. Last accessed Nov 2, 2021. https://www.weforum.org/agenda/2017/06/its-official-women-work-nearly-an-hour-longer-than-men-every-day/.

Piirto, Jane. "Synchronicity and Creativity." *Encyclopedia of Creativity* (Second Edition). (Cambridge: Academic Press, 2011), 409-413.

"Science of the Heart: Exploring the Role of the Heart in Human Performance: An Overview of Research Conducted by the HeartMath Institute." HeartMath Institute, Chapter 11. Last accessed Nov 2, 2021. https://www.heartmath.org/research/science-of-the-heart/intuition-research/.

Richardsson, Tanya Carroll. "6 Types of Spirit Guides & How To Communicate With Them." Mbgmindfulness. Last accessed Nov 2, 2021. https://www.mindbodygreen.com/0-17129/how-to-effectively-communicate-with-your-spirit-guides.html.

Raypole, Crystal. "Finding and Getting to Know Your Inner Child." Healthline. Last accessed Nov, 2, 2021. https://www.healthline.com/health/inner-child#takeaway.

Robbins, Jim. "How Immersing Yourself in Nature Benefits Your Health." Yale Environment 360. Last accessed Nov 2, 2021. https://e360.yale.edu/features/ecopsychology-how-immersion-in-nature-benefits-your-health.

Scuderi, Royale. "What Are the Differences Between Knowledge, Wisdom, and Insight?." Lifehack. https://www.lifehack.org/articles/communication/what-are-the-differences-between-knowledge-wisdom-and-insight.html.

Shen, Leonard, et al. "Body Wisdom and Mindfulness Tools to Enhance Workplace Performance" ABA 13TH Annual Labor and Employment

Conference November 9, 2019. https://www.americanbar.org/content/dam/aba/events/labor_law/2019/annual-conference/papers/body-wisdom-and-mindfulness.pdf.

"Success Starts With Self-Mastery: 7 Effective Strategies." Skip Richard. Last accessed Nov 2, 2021. https://www.skipprichard.com/success-starts-with-self-mastery-7-effective-strategies/.

The Gene Keys. Last accessed Nov 2, 2021. https://genekeys.com/.

Trieu, Tiffany. "What Is Inner Child Work? A Guide to Healing Your Inner Child." Mbgmindfulness. Last accessed Nov 2, 2021. https://www.mindbodygreen.com/articles/inner-child-work.

University of Rochester. "Spending time in nature makes people feel more alive, study shows." ScienceDaily. Last accessed November 1, 2021. https://www.sciencedaily.com/releases/2010/06/100603172219.htm.

University of Washington. "Regularly Immersing Yourself in Nature Can Help Health and Wellbeing." WUrban@UW. Last accessed Nov 2, 2021. https://depts.washington.edu/urbanuw/news/regularly-immersing-yourself-in-nature-can-help-health-and-wellbeing/.

Watts, Alan. "How your ego is affecting your mental health." iHASCO. Last accessed Nov 2, 2021. https://www.ihasco.co.uk/blog/entry/2206/get-to-know-your-ego.

WebMD Medical Reference. "What Is a People Pleaser?" WebMD. Last accessed Nov 2, 2021. https://www.webmd.com/mental-health/what-is-a-people-pleaser.

"What Is the Energy Body?." Just Be Well. Last accessed Nov 2, 2021. https://justbewell.info/what-is-the-energy-body/.

"What Success Means to Americans [Infographic]." Strayer University. Last accessed Nov 2, 2021. https://www.strayer.edu/buzz/what-success-means-americans-infographic.

Printed in Great Britain
by Amazon

17531740R00116